Distance Learners in Higher Education:

Institutional Responses for Quality Outcomes

Edited by
Chère Campbell Gibson

Atwood Publishing
Madison, Wisconsin

Cover design by Tamara Dever.

Distance Learners in Higher Education:
Institutional Responses for Quality Outcomes
by Chère Campbell Gibson
ISBN 1-891859-22-6

© 1998 Atwood Publishing
2710 Atwood Ave
Madison, WI 53704

Printed in the United States of America

02 01 00 99 ⎵ 8 7 6 5 4 3

Dedication

To distance learners...

Table of contents

Editor's notes

An interesting array of statistics has made a timely arrival on my desk over the last few weeks. The statistics that truly caught my attention came from the National Center for Educational Statistics, an arm of the U.S. Education Department, and were reported in *The Chronicle of Higher Education* in October 1997 on its Web site at:

http://chronicle.com/chedata/news.dir/dailarch.dir/9710.dir/97100703.htm

Based on a survey of a representative sample of 1,200 institutions of higher education in the United States, the study found that:

- Of the 14.3 million students enrolled in college in 1995-96, more than 750,000 were enrolled in distance education courses.

- Nearly one quarter of the 1,200 institutions in this nationally representative sample were offering degrees learners could pursue entirely at a distance.

- In the 1994-95 academic year, some 3,430 students received their degrees through distance education.

- By fall 1998, 90% of all institutions with 10,000 students or more and 85% of institutions with enrollments of 3,000 to 10,000 expect to be offering at least some distance education courses.

I'm not quite sure what shocked me more — the prevalence of distance education in higher education or the numbers of distance learners. What the statistics confirmed was that distance education and training is growing rapidly in higher education. However, as Tom Cyrs (1997) notes, "Many academic administrators act as though distance education was their field of dreams. Build the teleclassrooms, purchase the latest technology and the students will come." (p. 1)

Yes, the students will come, but one has to ask, will they succeed? To provide access to information is not the same as to ensure a successful learning experience! The analogy of assembling toys or garden equipment quickly comes to mind. You open the package, you review the bits and pieces, you read the instructions, and you're lost. And hope that a pony might emerge or that garden hose might one day uncoil from the scattered pieces is dashed. You can't understand the instructions, diagrams, and other aids. There's no one to call. Perhaps the author didn't understand your mechanical aptitude, appreciate your tool collection (or lack thereof), or recognize the pressure you'd be under during assembly.

If the distance learner is to succeed, we, as faculty, must do more than provide access to information. We need to truly understand that learner and design learning environments that facilitate learning, environments that enhance access to and success in higher education.

The authors, for this, the first book in the Atwood Publishing Diversity Series, were asked to reflect on current research and practices and address a specific facet of the distance learner to help us better understand this learner. Furthermore, they were asked to consider related implications for higher education. As you will note, the authors represent a variety of higher education institutions in North America and include both administrators and faculty. What becomes quickly obvious is their deep concern for learners and learning. What perhaps is less obvious is their years of research and practice in both credit and noncredit distance education.

One cautionary note: there is no need to read the book in any particular order. While I describe the contents in the order in which the chapters appear, I suggest you follow your own needs and interests. You might find it helpful to begin with Chapter One, which sets the stage with its discussion of the distance learner in higher education. But after that, the choice is yours. For those with very limited time, reading Chapter One followed by Chapter Nine, which summarizes the authors' recommendations, provides the quickest overview.

But if you decide to read from cover to cover, this is what you'll find. Following the Introduction by longtime friend and distance education scholar Michael G. Moore of The Pennsylvania State University, Melody Thompson, also of Penn State, provides an overview of the demographic, situational, and affective characteristics of the distance learner in higher education. She cautions us to remember that this is a very dynamic group of learners. In Chapter Two, Liz Burge of the University of New Brunswick helps us consider more specifically the role of gender in distance education, as she discusses the high proportion of women studying at a distance and the implications for facilitating learning and learner support.

Cultural considerations are highlighted in Chapter Three by Charlotte Gunawardena and Irene Sanchez of the University of New Mexico. Noting the breadth of cultural groups represented in the number of distance learners, they highlight learning style as a variable of concern. Focusing specifically on a case study of Hispanic distance learners, they note the implications of learning style on instructional design, teaching/learning, and support of the distance learner.

A discussion of the role of the learner's dynamic academic self-concept in learning and persistence in distance education, as well as the enhancers and detractors to this important concept, follows in Chapter Four by Chère Campbell Gibson of the University of Wisconsin-Madison. Chapter Five highlights learning strategies and distance learning, with a focus on learning strategically, as well as the roles of goals and motivation and their impact on learning outcomes. Chris Olgren, also of the University of Wisconsin-Madison, discusses the implications of learning strategies on instructional design, from initial information collected on the distance learner to assignment decisions and assessment.

Chapter Six, by Terry Anderson and Randy Garrison of the University of Alberta, highlights the changing roles of faculty and learners. With particular emphasis on learning in a networked world, the authors discuss learner control and responsibility as well as the learner's capabilities to assume responsibility to succeed at a distance. Multiple interaction types are noted, with a discussion of implications for design of instruction and learner support to enhance acquisition of new roles and responsibilities.

The distance learner in context provides the focus of Chapter Seven, in which Chère Campbell Gibson explores distance learners and the environment that surrounds them — family, work, leisure, community, etc.— and how this context may enhance or detract from a distance learner's success. The beginnings of a holistic concept of learner support are also discussed.

Chapter Eight, co-authored by Dan Granger of the University of Minnesota and Meg Benke of Empire State University, focuses on supporting the distance learner. They outline the development of a human infrastructure within the institution: support for the learner from initial inquiry about a course or degree program at a distance, through registration, financial and library support, to course completion, counseling for the next course, and graduation.

The book ends with a review and summary of key strategies to be considered in the design of instruction and the support of distance learners. In addition, a short bibliography is included, highlighting a list of journals and several Web sites that focus on teaching and learning at a distance.

Reference

Cyrs, T. (Ed.). (1997). Teaching and learning at a distance: What it takes to effectively design, deliver and evaluate programs. In *New Directions for Teaching and Learning*, No. 71. San Francisco: Jossey-Bass.

Introduction

Michael G. Moore

In the Editor's Notes with which this volume begins, Chère Campbell Gibson confronts college and university faculty with the following, apparently simple challenge: "If the distance learner is to succeed, we, as faculty, must do more than provide access to information. We need to truly understand that learner and design learning environments that facilitate learning..."

Thus the book addresses two simple questions. First, what do we know about the distance learner? Second, what do we know about helping that person to learn? And behind these questions lies a significant philosophical as well as methodological assertion, namely that we "must do more than provide access to information."

The group of writers Gibson has assembled to inform us on the issues involved in these two questions are those I would like, most respectfully, to describe as the new generation of leaders in the field of distance education.

They are all scholars, researchers, and teachers actively engaged in conceptualizing, shaping, and re-shaping North American distance education. Reshaping, because as everyone can see, the field is not what it was just five, let alone fifteen or fifty years ago. How could it be when

1

communication and communication technologies are changing so rapidly that leaders of nations declare that knowledge is an increasingly important factor of production, as vital for prosperity in the new millenium as land, labor, or capital? When, in what is now widely regarded as the "Information Age," continuing, life-long education is near the top of every nation's policy agenda and on the tip of every politician's tongue?

Never has the technology available to link learners and teachers been so powerful. Never have the opportunities of distance education been of greater interest and value. And, paradoxically, never has the gap of understanding between those who know how to design and deliver distance education programs of good quality and the policy-makers and administrators, both on our campuses as well as in our state and national capitals, who talk about the need for distance education but understand it so little — never has this gap been wider than it is today.

This leaves distance educators with a formidable task. Distance education scholars must do better in sharing their knowledge more widely and make the results of their research and practice better known. An important part of this is to explain their learner-centered approach, and to help conventional educators understand more about the complex process of designing, delivering, and supporting learning at a distance.

Why is it, we may ask, that postsecondary educators have so generally failed to study the learner with the same devotion with which they have studied the information they expect their students to study? Surely the learner is a fascinating phenomenon! Is it perhaps because the subject is really too difficult? Certainly I have always been impressed by the magnitude of the challenge of trying to understand a phenomenon that is not only a mixture of an infinite number of variables — emotional, intellectual, social, and physical — but also never the same from one day to another, one second to another. It does seem a daunting task.

And yet, before I turned to read what was written by the contributors Gibson has assembled here, I paused to ask myself, "Is it really so difficult?" Looking back over more than thirty years of observing distance learners around the world, I asked myself, what, if any, are the characteristics of the distant learner?

Well, first, these learners are of all races, both genders, and all ages. We find distance learners in Africa, Latin America, eastern as well as western Europe, and Asia. While some people emphasize the importance of cultural differences, and it is true that the teacher needs to take cultural norms into account when planning what to say, write, or do, and what to have the learners do, my own conclusion is that distant learners in one country are more like those in others than they are different. As for age, perhaps the younger adult is over-represented, and perhaps the really young students are somewhat more mature and thoughtful than their age-group peers. When distance learners are older, they are surprisingly youthful — like my oldest-ever student, a 92-year-old retired Welsh schoolteacher whose eyes glistened with excitement as he told me, "The world is full of wonderful things to do and to discover." But again, distance education methodologies do not seem to be more effective or applicable to one age group than to another.

Neither is the ability to benefit from distant learning greater within any social class or economic level, though I wouldn't question the common research finding that the person most likely to look for continuing education is one who already has some, and that person is more likely to be from a relatively advantaged background. On the other hand, I have worked with African farmers learning to change the ways they managed their crops, and civilians and military personnel learning such skills as automobile and aircraft maintenance. At the other extreme of the social scale, one of my favorite memories is talking with a distant learner I met on an airplane, who turned out to be the Lord Chancellor of England. My distance learners have included bishops, generals, bus drivers, homemakers, and at least a couple of convicted murderers. The only thing noticeable, really, is their diversity.

Did they have anything in common?

First, they all are remarkably motivated — which is typical of all distance learners (at least those who stay). While it is common for a significant proportion of the people in courses on a campus, at a workshop or a convention, or in other face-to-face teaching environments to be there for reasons that may not all seem directly related to learning, few people learn at a distance if they're not really committed to learning.

Second, with this high motivation to learn comes task orientation. Distance learners seem to be highly focused. They want to know clearly what they have to do, to know when and how the task must be completed, and (if they are convinced that the task is necessary) they then show steely determination to overcome all kinds of environmental and psychological impediments to accomplish it.

Third, the distance learner is usually forced to study in an environment less favorable to education, an environment that for some is nurturing of learning, but that for most is hostile. For every distance learner, it's an environment that is not specially dedicated to learning.

This brings us to the second part of Gibson's opening challenge. Our aim as faculty should be to focus our attention on making courses and other learning experiences that will best empower our students to learn, to learn fully, effectively, efficiently, and with rewarding satisfaction. It is the responsiblity of our profession to study ways of maximizing the potential of our environments to support their learning and to minimize those elements in their environments that may impede it.

I have already mentioned some of the conditions that characterize such courses. What all distant learners want, and deserve, is:

- Content that they feel is relevant to their needs
- Clear directions for what they should do at every stage of the course
- As much control of the pace of learning as possible
- A means of drawing attention to individual concerns
- A way of testing their progress and getting feedback from their instructors
- Materials that are useful, active, and interesting

While most learners, like people in general, have favorite communications technologies, it is rarely technology that determines how our learners feel about their distance learning programs. Whatever the technology used, what determines their satisfaction is the attention they receive from their teachers and from the system they work in to meet their needs as listed above. The process of designing programs that meet these needs, especially for large numbers of learners, dispersed over large areas, may be complex. The goal, however, is really very simple.

In her statement, "We, as faculty, must do more than provide access to information," Gibson has encapsulated one of the central problems facing not only distance educators, but all teachers and administrators. The problem of balancing content and process has become especially acute, as we all try to come to terms with the new possibilities for both that are offered by the communications technologies of the Information Age.

Not that this problem is a new one. On the contrary. For decades a substantial proportion of college and university faculty have conceived their role as limited to providing students with access to information. After all, they reason, if students have made it into our courses, they must have acquired the ability to study and process this information, and are responsible for their own learning. Access, in this context, usually has been a combination of "required reading" and oral presentation from the platform of the lecture hall. Other faculty, of course, took a contrasting view. With little or no training, and with often amateurish results, they invested time and effort in attempting to understand the optimal conditions under which learning would occur and to structure an environment in which students could benefit from their insights. They tried, often with little genuine encouragement from administration, to devise relationships between themselves and their students that would help each individual student process sterile information into personal knowledge.

Only in one part of the campus, however, have these goals of designing and constructing specific learner-friendly conditions for study been systematic, overt, conscious, and institutionalized. I refer, of course, to the distance learning programs. A distance education program should offer its students a course with clear, comprehensive, and exclusive statements of learning outcomes, its content trimmed to fit the student's time budget or shaped into hourly, daily, weekly, or monthly modules and units of study. A successful distance education program should have strategically placed, well-integrated testing and feedback mechanisms, with efficient individual learner-to-teacher communication channels and a mechanism for giving a student advice on learning-related personal difficulties. The weighing, vetting, and editing of every word printed, recorded, or filmed and monitoring teacher-learner exchanges is essential.

Of course, the list of standard design principles is much longer than this. My point in mentioning a few of them is to remind us of the existence of a well-tested body of knowledge about the methods that help students learn and the techniques of preparing environments more conducive to learning. Distance educators have become skillful in supporting learners while disseminating information.

And, as the authors of this book believe, it is very important that we in distance education develop our knowledge even further. It is also important, as so many faculty experiment with new Internet technologies, exploring them in ways and to a degree their predecessors never did with earlier technologies, that knowledge about facilitating learning at a distance be more widely understood by educators in general and be put into practice far more widely on campus as well as in distance environments.

A serious problem faces us in this regard. There is a real danger that, instead of seeing our campus colleagues adopt the learner-centered design and delivery methods traditional to distance education, we may experience the opposite. It is quite possible that the emerging generation of technology-aware campus faculty will not only use the new, information-rich technologies to reinforce the emphasis on information in their teaching, but will also, in their enthusiasm for the technology, become more involved in distance education and, in doing so, contribute to a reversal of the learner-centered techniques that have become traditional in our field.

Should this concern strike readers as far-fetched or alarmist, I invite them to review the proceedings of almost any conference that has "technology" or "distance learning" in its title. Consider the number and placement of presentations that demonstrate concern with the characteristics of learners or the processes of course design and learner support. Evaluate the extent to which conference planners promote complex technologies still in experimental form against the use of proven, cost-effective, and simpler technologies.

Consider, indeed, how frequently the terminology of distance learning is usurped to describe projects that have little to do with learning and nothing to do with distance learning — as understood by those who have studied the field, including the works of Wedemeyer, Holmberg, Keegan, or indeed the authors of this book.

We are fortunate to have a body of knowledge built by research, scholarship, and practice, built on the foundations of scholars such as these. However, the body of knowledge is increasingly hard to identify in the sandstorm of confused practice and promotion that passes for much of distance education in this "Information Age."

And yet, the new technology, more than any before, does offer the opportunity of balancing information with a well-designed and facilitated learning environment. This technology is not ready yet. In reality, at this moment, bandwidth limitations prevent us from providing through the Internet materials of the same technical quality as can be provided by a combination of print, audio and video recordings, and teleconferencing, whether video-, audio-, or computer-based. However, the technology will become available before too long. The skills of designing and delivering by means of traditional packages can then be transferred to design and delivery through the new medium. The question is whether educational administrators, those who control budgets and faculty reward systems, are able to capitalize on the knowledge of distance educators and to incorporate the learner-centered distance learning approach into the information-centered campus, or allow the reverse to take place. Another question is whether there can be better use of the knowledge of the relatively small field of academic distance educators.

This book will, I hope, make a significant contribution in this regard.

Chapter 1

Distance learners in higher education

Melody M. Thompson

Introduction

Only recently have learners become a major focus of study for the field of distance education. During the 1960s and '70s, as the field expanded and developed beyond the limits of correspondence study, most research efforts were centered on establishing the effectiveness and, it was hoped, the credibility of this form of education. When several decades of research provided overwhelming evidence of distance education's effectiveness as a delivery method (Moore and Thompson, 1997), educators began adding other, more student-focused questions to their research agendas, and the characteristics of students, particularly in relation to achievement in distance programs, became a major focus of study. This change in focus, which began with an emphasis on distance learners "as a sample population with group characteristics, i.e., flat, unchanging individuals" (Herrmann, 1988, p. 5), has expanded during the 1990s to accommodate a perception of the distance learner as a "dynamic individual" whose characteristics often change in response to both educational and life experiences (Gibson, 1992).

The dynamic nature of the individual learner is one obstacle to constructing a generic "profile" of the distance learner in higher education; the dynamic nature of the field of distance education is another. Increasingly, distance educators are describing a phenomenon variously referred to as "mainstreaming" or "convergence," that is, the gradual blurring of the distinction between conflicting "campus-bound" and "distance teaching" paradigms (OECD, 1996; Miller, 1997). One obvious consequence of the evolution to complementary "campus-based" and "distributed learning" paradigms (OECD, 1996) will be the concomitant blurring of the distinction between distance students and traditional students, a result that will have profound — but as yet unidentified — ramifications for research on students who study at a distance.

The selection of studies referred to below, although not exhaustive, represents a variety of perspectives on students in distance higher education. It is intended not to provide a static profile of a "typical" distance learner, but rather to offer an overview of both a dynamic population and the dynamic perspectives that distance educators are bringing to the study of those they serve.

Demographic and Situational Characteristics

As Holmberg (1995) points out, there "is no evidence to indicate that distance students should be regarded as a homogeneous group"; however, many distance students do share broad demographic and situational similarities that have often provided the basis for profiles of the "typical" distance learner in higher education. Characteristics included in such a profile have varied, but generally have reflected some combination of demographic and situational variables such as age, gender, ethnic background, disability, location, and life roles.

Age. Although the methods of reporting student ages vary from study to study, researchers agree that distance education students are, on average, older than typical undergraduate students. For example, a study of students enrolled in telecourses at four representative (urban, suburban, and rural) U.S. higher education institutions reported a median age of 36 (Hezel and Dirr, 1991). Dille and Mezack (1991) found that the average age of students enrolled in telecourses at a southwest (U.S.) community college was 27, while 80.3% of the students in Gibson and Graff's (1992) study of students in University of Wisconsin System Extended Degree programs were between 25 and 45. Robinson (1992) reports that almost half of the students enrolled in the Open College of Ryerson Polytechnical Institute in Ontario are between 31 and 46 years of age, and Wong (1992) notes that 83% of the distance education students at Memorial University of Newfoundland are 19 years of age or older. Finally, Holmberg (1995), citing studies from three decades, states that "the 25-35 age group seems to be the largest in most organizations." (p. 12)

Gender. Most studies of distance learners in North American higher education report that more women than men are enrolled in courses delivered at a distance. In telecourses at the four institutions examined by Hezel and Dirr (1991), 61% of the students were women. This finding is similar to that of Gibson and Graff (1992), who report that 60% of the students in their study were women. Dille and Mezack (1991) also found that women outnumbered men in the telecourses they examined; in their study, 71.5% of the respondents were female, a result comparable to that noted by Franks (1996), who reported that three-fourths of the distance education students at the College of Rural Alaska were female. Researchers studying distance education in Canada have reported similar findings: Robinson's (1991) study of distance students at the Open College of Ryerson Polytechnical Institute found that 77.9% were female, and at Athabasca University, 68% of the students and 63% of the graduates are women (Owen, 1991).

Comparative enrollment of women and men varies considerably in other parts of the world. Eastmond (1995) cites a 1992 study which reported that women outnumbered men in New Zealand and Israel, but that the opposite pattern existed in Britain, Germany, and Spain, perhaps reflecting cultural differences. A more recent report (Taylor and Kirkup, 1994) presents enrollment percentages for women in some of the larger distance education institutions: Open University, United Kingdom (50.0%); Indira Ghandi National Open University, India (26.0%); FernUniversität, Germany (27.4%); UNED, Spain (54.7%); and Open University, the Netherlands (38.0%).

Ethnic Background. Most reports in the literature focusing on the participation of students from various ethnic groups are program descriptions, rather than comparative studies. Although research studies occasionally report the percentages of participants from various ethnic backgrounds (e.g., Dille and Mezack, 1991; Pugliese, 1994), they generally do not compare these with the percentages of the same groups within the population of traditional students. As a result, making generalizations about the relative participation of ethnic minorities in distance education is difficult.

However, there is some evidence, largely qualitative and anecdotal, that distance education is a particularly appealing way for students from disadvantaged socio-economic groups to enter higher education. For many of these students, courses and programs delivered at a distance are an accessible avenue for upward mobility. For example, Eastmond (1995, p. 50) reports that all of the students in his study of a computer conferencing distance education program at a college for adult students represented the first generation in their families to obtain a higher education degree. In some cases, distance education "provides an opportunity for people without means ... to advance into more productive, satisfying lives." It can also offer a less threatening alternative to traditional educational structures for disadvantaged students whose earlier experiences in mainstream educational settings were unsatisfactory (Willis, 1994; Eastmond, 1995; Holmberg, 1995).

Disability. Keeping statistics on students with disabilities is difficult in the U.S. since federal law prohibits requiring students to identify themselves as disabled on application forms. Paist (1995) estimates that approximately 3% of in-state students enrolled in the University of Wisconsin-Extension Independent Study program have either visual, auditory, physical, or learning disabilities. She predicts that the percentage will increase steadily as more students discover the program's services and as the effects of the Americans with Disabilities Act spread. Vincent (1995) reports that approximately 5,000 of the undergraduates (about 5%) at Open University of the United Kingdom have disabilities; this number is increasing at the rate of about 10% per year, a rate higher than that of the general increase in enrollments. Vincent ascribes this growth to the convenience of home study and the ability of information technology to overcome barriers to learning for disabled students.

Location. Traditionally, distance education has attracted students whose geographic distance from a higher education institution discouraged or prevented enrollment in on-campus classes. The students in Gibson and Graff's (1992) study are typical of this group: 77% lived over fifty-one miles from campus, with the majority living between 101 and 200 miles from campus. Recent data on extended campus enrollments in Colorado also reflect this phenomenon with the report that "residents of rural counties enrolled in extended campus courses at substantially higher rates than urban residents" (Statewide Extended Campus, 1996).

However, in many institutions the "typical" distance learner is no longer place-bound. Increasingly, students in close geographical proximity to traditional educational institutions are choosing distance study not because it is the only alternative, but rather because it is the preferred alternative. Hezel and Dirr (1991), for example, found that 56% of the telecourse students they surveyed reported a one-way potential commute of thirty minutes or less, and Robinson (1992) reported that more than 67% of the distance students in his study lived within 50 miles of the Open College. Students' motivations for choosing distance study even when traditional study is available will be discussed below.

Life Roles. In addition to filling the role of student, most distance learners also fill the roles of worker and spouse. A number of studies reporting characteristics of distance learners have documented the extent of this trend. St. Pierre and Olsen (1991), for example, found that 57% of the students in their study worked 40 or more hours a week outside the home. Robinson (1992) reported that among distance education students at the Open College, 83.7% were employed outside the home (62.2% full time) and 58.5% were married. Over 90% of the students in the Gibson and Graff (1992) study were employed (75.8% full time) and approximately 75% were married. In Fjortoft's (1996) study of a post-baccalaureate program in pharmacy, 78% of the respondents reported working more than 40 hours/week and the majority were married. Among those interviewed by Eastmond (1995) in his study of distance students at Hawks College, all were employed, 90% were employed full time, and 75% were married. These numbers not only illustrate significant differences between distance students and their on-campus counterparts, but also go far to explain the appeal of distance education programs. The convenience and flexibility offered by programs free of the constraints of place — and often time, as well — represent major benefits to learners attempting to juggle multiple adult roles and responsibilities.

The studies cited here and other similar reports have provided the basis for a widely accepted view of the distance learner as one who is (1) older than the typical undergraduate, (2) female, (3) likely to be employed full time, and (4) married. Some researchers in the field have used this profile as the basis for studying the relationship between specific student characteristics and student success in distance education programs.

Relationship of Demographic Characteristics to Student Success

Research attempting to measure the relationship of particular demographic characteristics to student success — as measured by levels of persistence and/or achievement — has resulted in often contradictory conclusions. Some studies have reported no correlation between these outcomes and specific demographic variables such as gender (e.g., Dille and Mezack, 1991; Fjortoft, 1996), ethnic background (Dille and Mezack, 1991), or age (Powell, Conway, and Ross, 1990; Gibson and Graff, 1992). Other studies suggest that certain demographic variables, perhaps not in and of themselves but rather as the markers of an accompanying set of generalized characteristics, are related to student success and/or satisfaction.

For example, several researchers reporting a positive relationship between success and students' age (Dille and Mezack, 1991; Souder, 1994) have explained the higher levels of success for older students on the basis of the increased maturity, self-discipline, life experience, and financial responsibility for their educations that are likely to characterize older students. Additionally, older students are more likely to have higher levels of education at the time of enrollment, another factor which has been correlated with success (Dille and Mezack, 1991; Gibson and Graff, 1992).

Higher success rates among female distance education students have been related to (1) the lower proportion of women working full time outside the home, (2) the higher rates at which women access institutional support structures, (3) the potentially higher level of motivation that might operate among women, who more often work in occupational sectors in which career advancement is closely tied to academic upgrading, and (4) the appeal of the distance format to woman who must integrate education into lives characterized by multiple roles (Ross and Powell, 1990; Powell, Conway, and Ross, 1990; Robinson, 1992).

Affective Characteristics of Distance Learners

Whereas earlier research on learner characteristics focused on demographics and life situation, the last ten years have seen a shift in attention to the affective characteristics of students in distance education programs. However, much of the literature continues to reflect a desire to develop a "profile" — albeit a more comprehensive profile — of the distance learner, specifically in terms of personality type, learning styles, and motivation.

Personality Type. Recent research on characteristics of distance learners has frequently focused on personality variables associated with partici-

14

pation and/or success in distance education programs. As Biner et al. (1995) explain, the term "personality" refers to "the cognitions, the emotions, and the behaviors ... that remain relatively stable across time and situations." Several authors have noted a "cluster of [personality] characteristics" that seem to accompany preference for and success in distance education programs, e.g., autonomy, tolerance for ambiguity, and flexibility (Willis, 1994, p. 54; Eastmond, 1995). Studies providing the basis for this characterization have focused on single attributes, such as students' locus of control or orientation toward self-direction, as well as on more complete personality profiles.

Internal locus of control — the belief that consequences stem from one's own behaviors and efforts — appears to be an attribute of many students who choose to study at a distance, particularly for those who are successful in their programs. A study comparing the personality variables of undergraduate education students enrolled in independent study with those receiving conventional instruction found that the students studying at a distance were more likely to have an internal locus of control than were their on-campus peers (Jonassen and Grabinger, 1988). Dille and Mezack (1991) reported that internal locus of control was positively correlated with success in community college distance learning courses. Alternatively, external locus of control and a related construct, external attribution, have been reported to characterize at-risk distance education students (Dille and Mezack, 1991; Kember et al., 1991). A more recent study by Pugliese (1994) found that, while external locus of control was the strongest predictor for withdrawal/failure, the relationship was not significant.

Another characteristic of interest to researchers is self-directedness, since common sense suggests that students separated from their instructor would benefit from this attribute. Billings (1993) reviewed studies that examined students' orientation toward self-directed learning and self-management. Results were mixed, with several studies suggesting a positive relationship between self-directedness and achievement and several others reporting no relationship between the ability to manage one's own learning and academic success. A study to examine the applicability of the concept of self-directedness to distance learners at the Open College (Robinson, 1992, p. 13) found that students "were not interested in self-directed learning. They wanted explicit directions on how to do the assignments, and for the course designer to select the assignments for grading." The investigator speculates that this lack of interest may reflect (1) the lack of need for such an approach given the

15

highly structured nature of the courses, (2) a perception of self-directed-ness as too time-consuming, or (3) learners' lack of experience in directing their own learning projects.

Biner et al. (1995, p. 56) found that the personality profile of college-level telecourse students differed considerably from that of traditional students, as reflected in the Sixteen Personality Factor Questionnaire (16PF). Specifically, students in the distance education programs tended to be "more intelligent, emotionally stable, trusting, compulsive, passive, and conforming" than traditional students. Several personality factors were found to predict success in the distance context: self-sufficiency and/or introversion, laxness (i.e., carelessness of social rules), and expediency were all associated with successful student performance.

Learning Style. Billings (1993, p. 2) defines learning style as "the way in which a learner receives and interacts with instruction and responds to the learning environment." Most of the research conducted on learning style preferences and distance learners has focused on the apparent effects of particular preferences on student success. Coggins (1989), for example, found a negative correlation between the need for both peer and instructor affiliation and course completion. Dille and Mezack (1991) reported that students with lower means on the Concrete Experience Scale of Kolb's Learning Style Inventory and with higher scores on the AC-CE (Abstract Conceptualization minus Concrete Experience) Scale were more likely to succeed in their telecourses. These results suggest that (1) successful students have less need to relate to others in the educational environment and (2) a less concrete learning style is better suited to telecourse learning.

Another study (Gibson and Graff, 1992) used the Canfield Learning Style Inventory (CLSI) to examine differences between successful and unsuc-cessful students in terms of learning style preferences and perception of barriers to participation and/or success. Analysis of the four major areas measured by this scale — preferred conditions, content, modes, and expectancy of performance — resulted in significant differences between successful and unsuccessful students (in this study defined as completers and noncompleters, respectively). Results of the study indicated that successful students exhibited lower levels of peer affiliation and higher levels of confidence in their performance and competence, while non-completers exhibited higher peer affiliation and less confidence in their knowledge, skills, and ability to reach their goal of degree completion.

Most students' learning styles are characterized by perceptual prefer-ences, that is, preferences for the sensory channels through which they receive information. Although several studies have examined this char-acteristic of distance learners, none has suggested a preference that characterizes distance learners in general. Most attempts to relate audi-tory, tactile, or visual preferences to achievement have had similar results, reporting no significant relationship between these preferences and achievement or success (Coggins, 1989; McFarland, 1990; Billings and Cobb, 1992). One exception is a study by Jonassen and Grabinger (1988), which found that undergraduate students electing independent study preferred learning via active or hands-on experimentation.

Motivations. Some motivations for studying at a distance can best be understood in terms of the barriers that block students from enrolling in on-campus courses. Thus, many students are motivated to become dis-tance learners because the barrier of geographic distance from the nearest or most appropriate institution makes conventional study impractical. Hezel and Dirr's (1991) study of barriers to on-campus attendance found that distance from campus was viewed as "very important" or "somewhat important" by 75% of the students surveyed; understandably, this factor was more of a problem for students in rural areas.

Being place-bound continues to motivate many students, especially adult students whose life situations make either relocating to the site of an educational institution or even attending a nearby institution impractical. Increasingly, however, researchers are finding that the motivation that comes from being place-bound is being superseded in importance by that which comes from being time-bound.

Of the community college telecourse students surveyed regarding per-ceived barriers to on-campus attendance, 95% identified time constraints as a "very important" or "somewhat important" barrier (Hezel and Dirr, 1991). This finding is similar to that of Liviertos and Franks (1996), who reported that 82% of students surveyed identified lack of time for on-campus attendance as a very important motivation for enrolling in a telecourse. Factors contributing to the sense of being time-bound include work, family, and community responsibilities (Willis, 1994; *Going the Distance*, 1994; Hyatt, 1992).

To the motivations of access and flexibility already discussed, Willis (1994) adds a third motivation for distance study: attraction to innovative learning environments. For some students, distance learning represents not merely an acceptable replacement, but rather a desirable alternative to on-campus instruction. Reasons for desiring to be outside the educational mainstream might include negative past experiences with conventional education, preference for independent study, or attraction to a technological environment (Willis, 1994; Eastmond, 1995).

Goals

Since the majority of distance learners are time-bound adults with multiple roles and responsibilities, it is not surprising that most have educational goals that are instrumental rather than developmental. Among the 2,300 FernUniversität students surveyed by von Prümmer (1990), the three most frequently mentioned goals were work-related. Attaining an advanced professional qualification was mentioned by 84.4% of the students, exposure to new professional perspectives by 80.9%, and gaining specialized knowledge by 78.6%. Goals relating to general knowledge ranked fourth through seventh and ninth.

Robinson (1992) found that most students at the Open College had instrumental goals, such as increased knowledge of a specific content area or performing more effectively in some aspect of their lives. Only three of the twenty students studied by Eastmond (1995) had goals that were personal or academic; all of the others had career development as their goal. Within this career-orientation group, Eastmond identified three categories of degree seekers: "necessity learners," who need a degree to maintain their positions, advance in their current situation, or prepare for a new job; "recareerers/ladder climbers," whose external necessity is not as compelling, but who nevertheless have a goal that will be facilitated by further education; and "rainy day planners," who are using further education as protection against unforeseen contingencies in their current work situation.

Several studies have reported significant differences between men's and women's rankings of goals. Von Prümmer (1990) reported that for women in her study "opening up new areas of knowledge" was the most frequently identified goal; it was chosen by 84.0% of the women, compared with 73.4% of the men. For men, the most frequently identified goal was "higher professional qualification," which was chosen by 85.4% of the men and 82.5% of the women. Further, women more often identified proving themselves and increasing their self-esteem as important goals than did men (63.9% vs. 53.9%). They also reported being more interested in "intellectual stimulation" (74.1% vs. 56.8%) and making up for earlier lack of opportunities (55.4% vs. 45.7%).

Among students at Athabasca University, more women than men rated gaining a university degree as highly important (Ross and Powell, 1990). Additionally, more women than men reported studying for self-improvement and intellectual stimulation rather than for higher professional qualifications (Owen, 1991). Robinson (1992) found no gender-based differences in goals among distance education students at the Open College.

A Dynamic Conception
of the Distance Learner

Although the attempt to develop a profile of the distance learner in higher education has broadened beyond demographics to include affective characteristics as well, the goal of a composite representation of the "typical" student has remained largely unrealized. To those looking for a way to easily identify target populations or to design broadly appropriate programs, the elusiveness of this goal is probably disappointing. However, two things are immediately obvious from any more-than-superficial examination of the literature: (1) the distance learner population is — and will continue to be — too heterogeneous to provide a basis for a "typical" profile, and (2) even for an individual learner, any profile must be tentative and dynamic, rather than static.

Although the proportions of students sharing particular demographic and situational characteristics have been high enough to encourage general descriptions of distance learners, they have not been high enough to support development of profiles that can guide the design of uniform programs appropriate for a "general audience" of distance learners. The increasing emphasis within the field on meeting individual needs, and the aforementioned convergence of distance education practice and campus-based instruction argue against both the desirability and the possibility of developing anything approaching a standardized description of — or programs for — *the* distance learner.

A strong case for the tentative and dynamic nature of any profile purporting to represent even an individual distance learner is steadily being developed by researchers in the field. A number of recent studies have examined the changing nature of learner characteristics and have discussed implications for practice. Powell, Conway, and Ross (1990), for example, discuss the interplay of students' predisposing characteristics (those relatively fixed characteristics initially brought to the educational activity), changing life circumstances, and institutional factors. Other researchers have focused on changes in students' self-perceptions as they progress through their programs (Herrmann, 1988; Gibson, 1992, 1996) and on changes in students' willingness and ability to exercise control and/or self-direction (Kasworm and Yao, 1992; Garland, 1994). Understanding of the dynamic nature of distance learner characteristics has profound implications for program design, instruction, and learner support.

Conclusion

A close examination of the demographic, situational, and affective characteristics of those who study at a distance reveals both similarities common to large proportions of the population as well as a wide range of individual characteristics and, therefore, needs. This growing understanding of distance education students as diverse and dynamic individuals occurs within an educational context increasingly characterized by a focus on providing "learner-centered" education.

The institutional mandate that is emerging from the convergence of these phenomena is one of equity, not equality: to appropriately serve distance learners, institutions must offer programs designed for learners with a wide range of characteristics and needs, not for a hypothetical "typical" student. Because "distance education in the twenty-first century must mean education any time, anywhere, for anyone," the paradigm of equal "education for all" must give way to that of appropriate "education for each" (Dillon and Blanchard, 1992, p. 29). The ability of educational institutions to fulfill their responsibility of appropriately serving a diverse population of distance learners will depend both on the knowledge gained from further student-centered research and on the flexible programming and learner support systems made possible by current and emerging distance education technologies.

References

Billings, D. (1993). Learning style preferences and distance education: A review of literature and implications for research. In *Distance Education Symposium: Selected Papers, Part 2* (ACSDE Research Monograph No. 4), 1-11. University Park, PA: The American Center for the Study of Distance Education, The Pennsylvania State University.

Billings, D., & Cobb, N. (1992). Effects of learning style preference, attitude, and GPA on learning using computer-assisted instruction and the traditional lecture method. *Computers in Nursing*, 7(4), 152-56.

Biner, P., Bink, M. L., Huffman, M. L., & Dean, R. S. (1995). Personality characteristics differentiating and predicting the achievement of televised-course students and traditional-course students. *The American Journal of Distance Education*, 9(2), 46-60.

Coggins, C. C. (1989). Preferred learning styles and their impact on the completion of external degree programs. *The American Journal of Distance Education*, 2(1), 25-37.

Dille, B., & Mezack, M. (1991). Identifying predictors of high risk among community college telecourse students. *The American Journal of Distance Education*, 5(1), 24-35.

Dillon, C., & Blanchard, D. (1992). Education for each: Learner driven distance education. *Distance Education Symposium: Selected Papers, Part 1* (ACSDE Research Monograph No. 4), 9-33. University Park, PA: American Center for the Study of Distance Education, The Pennsylvania State University.

Eastmond, D. V. (1995). *Alone but together: Adult distance study through computer conferencing.* Cresskill, NJ: Hampton Press.

Fjortoft, N. F. (1996). Persistence in a distance learning program: A case in pharmaceutical education. *The American Journal of Distance Education*, 10(3), 49-59.

Franks, K. (1996). Attitudes of Alaskan distance education students toward media and instruction. *The American Journal of Distance Education*, 10(3), 60-74.

Garland, M. R. (1994). The adult need for "personal control" provides a cogent guiding concept for distance education. *Journal of Distance Education*, IX(1), 45-59.

Gibson, C. C. (1992). Changing perceptions of learners and learning at a distance: A review of selected recent research. *Distance Education Symposium: Selected Papers, Part 1* (ACSDE Research Monograph No. 4), 34-42. University Park, PA: American Center for the Study of Distance Education, The Pennsylvania State University.

Gibson, C. C. (1996). Toward an understanding of academic self-concept in distance education. *The American Journal of Distance Education*, 10(1), 23-36.

Gibson, C. C., & Graff, A. O. (1992). Impact of adults' preferred learning styles and perception of barriers on completions of external baccalaureate degree programs. *Journal of Distance Education*, VII(1), 39-51.

Going the Distance. (1994). Washington, DC: The Annenberg/CPB Project.

Herrmann, A. (1988). A conceptual framework for understanding the transitions of perceptions of external students. *Distance Education*, 9(1), 5-26.

Hezel, R., & Dirr, P. (1991). Understanding television-based distance education: Identifying barriers to university attendance. *Research in Distance Education*, 3(1), 2-5.

Holmberg, B. (1995). *Theory and practice of distance education.* New York: Routledge.

Hyatt, S. (1992, May). Developing and managing a multi-model distance learning program in the two-year college. Paper presented at the Annual International Conference of the National Institute for Staff and Organizational Development on Teaching Excellence, Austin, TX. (ERIC Document Reproduction Service ED 349-009).

Jonassen, D. H., & Grabinger, R. S. (1988). Independent study: Personality, cognitive, and descriptive predictors. (ERIC Document Reproduction Service ED 295 641).

Kasworm, C. E., & B. Yao. (1992, November). The development of adult learner autonomy and self-directedness in distance education. Paper presented at the World Conference of the International Council for Distance Education, Bangkok, Thailand. (ERIC Document Reproduction Service ED 355 453).

Kember, D., Murphy, D., Siaw, I., & Yuen, K.S. (1991). Towards a causal model of student progress in distance education: Research in Hong Kong. *The American Journal of Distance Education*, 5(2), 3-15.

Liviertos, B., & Frank, J. (1992). Alternative learning modes: Spring '92 telecourse and Weekend College Enrollees. Columbia, MD: Howard Community College Office of Planning and Evaluation Research. (ERIC Document Reproduction Service ED 385 311).

McFarland, M. (1990). An analysis of the relationship between learning style perceptual preferences and attitudes toward computer-assisted instruction. Paper delivered at the 8th Annual Meeting of the National League for Nursing, Council for Research in Nursing Education, San Francisco, CA.

Miller, G. (1997). Research opportunities in distance education. *PAACE Journal of Lifelong Education*, 6, 1-7.

Organization for Economic Cooperation and Development, OECD Proceedings. (1996). *Adult Learning in a New Technological Era*. Paris: OECD Publications.

Owen, M. (1991). Who benefits from distance education? A study of Athabasca University graduates, 1985-1990. Draft paper. (ERIC Document Reproduction Service ED 341 301).

Paist, E. (1995). Serving students with disabilities in distance education programs. *The American Journal of Distance Education*, 9(1), 61-70.

Powell, R., Conway, C., & Ross, L. (1990). Effects of student predisposing characteristics on student success. *Journal of Distance Education* , V(1), 5-19.

Pugliese, R. R. (1994). Telecourse persistence and psychological variables. *The American Journal of Distance Education*, 8(3), 22-39.

Robinson, R. (1992). Andragogy applied to the Open College learner. *Research in Distance Education*, 4(1), 10-13.

Ross, L., & Powell, R. (1990). Relationships between gender and success in distance education courses: A preliminary investigation. *Research in Distance Education*, 2(2), 10-11.

St. Pierre, S., & Olsen, L.K. (1991). Student perspectives on the effectiveness of correspondence instruction. *The American Journal of Distance Education*, 5(3), 65-71.

Souder, W. E. (1994). The effectiveness of traditional vs. satellite delivery in three Management of Technology master's degree programs. *The American Journal of Distance Education* , 7(1), 37-53.

Statewide Extended Campus. (1996). Report on Colorado Statewide Extended Studies Program. (ERIC Document Reproduction Service ED 396 626).

Taylor, L., & Kirkup, G. (1994). From the local to the global: Wanting to see women's participation and progress at the OUUK in a wider context. *Open Praxis* , 1, 12-14.

Vincent, T. (1995). Information technology and disabled students. Overcoming barriers to learning. In F. Lockwood (Ed.), *Open and distance learning today* , pp. 87-97. London: Routledge.

von Prümmer, C. (1990). Study motivation of distance students. *Research in Distance Education*, 2(2), 2-6.

Willis, B. (1994). *Distance education: Strategies and tools.* Englewood Cliffs, N.J: Educational Technology Publications .

Wong, S. (1992). Approaches to study of distance education students. *Research in Distance Education*, 4(3), 11-17.

Chapter 2

Gender in distance education

Elizabeth Burge

Hear the voices of three female graduate students:

> Problem-solving, for me, is very difficult, as is forming my own theory or concept when learning. It seems to me everyone has valid points and they're not to be disputed, and if I were to, then I possibly would start World War III. I do need to develop my critical thinking and individuation without fear of hurting everyone. Maybe if I weren't a woman I wouldn't have such a hard time with this issue .... Even though I come to class quite motivated, I fear voicing my ideas, I fear potential failure, I fear the facilitator ... I feel dumb, I feel as if I'm not learning as much as the others seem to be (D, 1997, p. 8, 4).

> Indeed, I am awed by male students' behaviour who act as if they have the learning world by the tail. This is so foreign to my thinking that it leaves me alienated and wondering, among other things, how long it will be until the professors discover that I am actually stupid (J, 1997, p. 8).

> Returning to university ... is viewed by myself as a personal journey and one that I have waited too long to pursue. It is a personal goal set by myself which is independent of my being

a wife, a mother, employee, etc. This is my fourth attempt to obtain a Master's degree since age 20, and I encountered difficulties ... and ... obstacles which prevented my participation. I often had to remind myself that these were just temporary setbacks and could be overcome with time. ... [My] Situational barriers included lack of finances and the demands of raising young children. Dispositional barriers [included] societal and family attitudes about a young mother and new wife becoming a student, which affected my view of myself as a learner ... (K, 1997, p. 3).

These voices are almost everyday sounds in my distance education landscape. I hear and see too many examples of highly intelligent female students referring to challenges around their identity and inclusion in the academic world.

This chapter therefore uses my own experience in distance teaching and the research literature to explore the key challenges regarding gender issues in distance-mode higher education classrooms. It also offers summary guidelines to address the key issues raised by these and other voices: participation, curricula, barriers, and technology application. The guidelines refer to constructivist ways of learning, woman-friendly teaching strategies, and policy guidelines regarding equitable use of the new technologies, especially the Internet.

But first some background factors that inform my practice.

Author Background

I work in a mid-sized Canadian university, which our new president is taking through a 'right-sizing' process: she says that we have to "do the right things with less." Part of the "lessness" is reduced support staff help, so I look for all the shortcuts and efficiencies I can find.

Surrounding me is what feels like a technologically deterministic environment: "a new technology is seen as something whose 'time has come' ... technology seems beyond our influence" (Cockburn and Ormrod, 1993, p. 8). I am told by some people that technology provides many solutions for current educational problems and that I should accept the impacts of technology as a necessary change to my everyday existence. Most of these folks are the early and enthusiastic adopters of technology (and most often male). I feel the pressures of the new technology and the assumptions about its use. My graduate students experience similar pressures.

My teaching experience using non-lecture methods in audio-, video-, and computer-conferencing reinforces my belief in the need to first interrogate every technology from a learner's viewpoint (Burge, 1996). Reassuring numbers of experienced distance education colleagues tell me they use similar critical approaches, found in such questions as these:

- It moves data, but does it move minds?

- It collects learners into a group, but does it connect them into a productive process?

- It's a big wide highway, but who cannot get on to it?

- It offers great solutions, but where does reality meet the rhetoric?

All our (adult) M. Ed. learners want to experience efficiently managed and productive formal classrooms and home learning environments. Many of them use distance-mode classrooms because we tend to teach in the convergence model. That is, in each class I have learners sitting literally around me in a walled classroom and metaphorically around me across the province in special audio-conference facility sites. We get into Internet use more slowly, because of learner access and cost problems and our policy of nondiscrimination based on technology access.

Many students adapt easily and well to interacting with each other without the usual paralinguistic cues for conversation. All of us regard the three-hour class times as valuable. Learners incur financial and other costs in just getting to class, as does the university in setting up the communications technologies and facilities. Therefore, class time is not wasted on transmitting information to relatively open and passive minds. Paper does a better and cheaper job. Learners come to class prepared to analyze, apply, and critique the information they have studied prior to class.

Time and other costs are not the only reason for this teaching model: I try to follow a constructivist approach to learning (Fosnot, 1996; Wilson, 1995). Therefore I try to listen more than I speak, so that I can get a sense of how learners build their mental frameworks, how they act as their own knowledge architects, not as photocopy machines. I try to speak on average for less than 30% of the total time in class. Communications technologies, in my experience, tend to amplify faculty teaching and learners' learning skills and weaknesses, especially in contexts where people cannot see each other. So self-discipline, attention to group process, and a defined but relaxed 'presence' online are needed to develop a comfortable, productive environment.

After doing some initial design work last year to render an Internet software programme appropriate for the communicative and cognitive demands of master's level courses, and feeling some excitement over such ownership of creative thinking, my graduate students and I were then excluded from further design work when the computing specialists took over (Burge and Carter, 1997). Their product was revised after a reluctant admission that they should have kept the users as part of the design team.

There is a lesson here for administrators and academic leaders who wish to encourage more faculty to use new technologies and adapt teaching styles to less transmissive models. The exercise reminded me of Bryson and de Castell's (1995, p. 22) point that historically the relationship of women to technology suggests in part that "women are usually involved in the development and/or early uses of technologies, then squeezed out as 'expertise' coalesces around male expertise, and attendant social relations and practices are redistributed."

Enough of my context. It is now time to highlight gender issues in distance education, using the term "gender" in its basic meaning of the socially constructed definitions of roles and behaviours for women and men. Gender as a concept has

> proved such a powerful explanatory theory that by the 1980's it was being used to explain the way knowledge ... and inanimate aspects of the material world such as technology ... and physical space ... were "gendered" (Kirkup, 1996, p. 147).

Women in Distance Education

First, some statistics and a little history. Distance education continues to offer women opportunities to enrich their lives and expand their earning power. Comprehensive accurate statistics are not yet available on women learning through distance education. But we do know so far that most distance learners are women, but also that many are still under-represented in many distance-mode programs and that gendering of course choices is evident.

Statistics Canada, for example, reported recently that 60%-70% of the estimated 400,000 distance learners in Canada are female (Normand, 1995). Kirkup and von Prümmer (1997, p. 43) report that, for the period

1990-1992, women account for 50.0% of the undergraduate students in the British Open University, 54.7% in the Spanish distance teaching university, 38.0% in the Netherlands equivalent, and 31.0% in the German one. Yet von Prümmer (1997) found that the FernUniversität, Germany's distance-mode university, "is not geared to the situation of women with their double or triple workload at home and in paid work, and ignores the learning styles of women." Gendered course choices are seen, for example, in The Open University (UK) where, based on 1994 figures,

> Women are over represented in the traditionally female areas of the curriculum: arts and education, and poorly represented in traditionally male areas: technology and maths. This gendering is even stronger in other programmes. Women make up ... 81 percent of students on health and social welfare courses ... only 11 percent ... in computers and manufacturing postgraduate programmes (Kirkup and von Prümmer, 1997, p. 44).

I suspect that similar gender-based differences could be seen in North America, as well. Accurate current Canadian statistics are elusive, particularly as so many "regular" institutions now offer distance-mode programs and they show great variance in their record-keeping. Nevertheless, the numbers of women distance students and their fee-paying power are not to be discounted.

Serious research attention to female distance learners began in the late 1970s. Since then, when Aisla Swarbrick in England focused on women's access to technology, we have seen a great variety in topics studied.

The first published compilation of practice and research about women distance learners (Faith, 1988) discussed the impact on learning of women's multiple life burdens, access to courses and resources, learner support services, gender bias in language and course materials, education for social and educational advancement, epistemology, curriculum design, teaching practice, and the needs of specialist groups of learners, e.g., aboriginals. Gill Kirkup summed up with style the book's themes of inclusion and identity:

> We don't simply want to make higher education a place where more women are more comfortable; we want to change the nature of what has previously constituted the disciplines so that we are in the content as well as in the institution. ... Or in the case of distance education, in the text as well as in the armchair studying it (Kirkup, 1988, p. 287).

Since 1988, we have seen increasing but still relatively small numbers of articles and research studies (e.g., Burge, 1990; Coates, 1994; Evans, 1995; Grace, 1991; Lunneborg, 1994; Pravda, 1994; Smith and Norlen, 1994; Spronk, 1994; Taylor and Kirkup, 1994; Umeå Universitet, 1993; von Prümmer, 1997, 1993). The writings selected from distance education literature show current thinking about gender in distance education as it relates to participation, curriculum and learning designs, barriers to learning, and the use of technologies.

The earliest days of consciousness-raising about women's issues in distance education (early 1980s) showed female faculty explaining, for example, how power and epistemological biases operate through sexist language and in certain theories about the world, and how distance education may reinforce the domestication of educational labour and the isolation of women (Faith, 1988).

Various articles in the Canadian-based *Journal of Distance Education* have spoken directly to gender issues (e.g., Burge and Lensjky, 1990; Kirkup and von Prümmer, 1990; May, 1994; Moran, 1990). Gill Kirkup and Christine von Prümmer (1990), for example, explained how women's needs for "connectedness" in their learning are indications of difference in learning style, not deficit in cognition. Women's writings about distance education experience and their references to the now classic research about women's moral development with its ethics of caring and compassion (compared with male ethics of rights and rules) (Gilligan, 1982) and the landmark "women's ways of knowing" research (Belenky, Clinchy, Goldberger, and Tarule, 1986) helped reduce the assumed conceptual and practical power of two key terms used by many male writers in distance education — independence and autonomy.

And as communications technologies became more popular, we talked more about how to connect learners into productive discussion groups. Barbara Spronk has reinforced the point about connection, but with a warning particular to women's lives. She echoes the voices of the three women who opened this chapter:

> The spaces women occupy are crowded with connections, bonds and obligations that we have been taught to welcome and cherish, so much so that we find ourselves having to un-learn this pattern so that we can make a bit more room for ourselves (1990, p. 11).

Participation

Participation statistics and behaviours have been studied in European contexts by Kirkup and von Prümmer, thus increasing our awareness of the psychological, time, and economic burdens carried by working women who want simultaneously to study, hold down a job, and manage a household. Von Prümmer (1993, p. 62) reported that many female distance learners experience another kind of double burden, the additional demands from their family and their own self-imposed, sometimes dysfunctionally high standards for "domestic and mothering roles," as if they want to offer compensation for "being allowed" to enter formal programs.

Many women students also experience less than ideal study conditions; hear one telling the Convocation audience at Athabasca University in 1988 how she managed her study times:

> In self-defense I developed study habits which I'm sure no one [at the university] would even remotely recommend. ... I opened my books first thing in the morning and studied five minutes here, five minutes there, from morning till night, as my family and friends devised schemes to ensure I never had an hour of solid study time (Johnson, 1988, p. 2).

'Special' programs to increase women's access to education and dilute the gendering factor in course selection have focused on building technology, management, information technology, and law (Faith, 1988; Kirkup and von Prümmer, 1997). Courses with content that is closer to traditionally assumed interests of women, e.g., nursing, teaching, and women's studies, have also been reported in the distance education literature, with emphasis on the conditions needed for effective learning by female students.

Curriculum

Learning designs appropriate to women continue to be discussed, but not yet with enough attention to technology application. Writers, including the three female students at the beginning of the chapter, emphasize the 'difference not deficit' factors in women's learning and the effects of gender socialization on women's expectations of success (Faith, 1988).

When educators impose culturally alienating assumptions about prior life experiences, pay inadequate attention to frequent and easy access to resources, ignore different "ways of knowing" found in women's epistemologies, or design competitive or 'alone' types of learning activities, they may drive many women away from programs or drive them into inappropriate academic street-smarts (e.g., 'anything to get my degree'). Such results do not help financially challenged educational institutions to buy client loyalty in today's competitive marketplace.

Distance education discussions about women's learning add to the already large body of research into women's learning in "traditional" walled classrooms (e.g., Gabriel and Smithson, 1990; Gaskell and Willinsky, 1995; Maher and Tetrault, 1994), into the preferred relational styles of many female learners (compared with the autonomous styles preferred by many male learners) (MacKeracher, 1996), and the ways in which women come to know what they know (Goldberger, Tarule, Clinchy, and Belenky, 1996; Belenky, Clinchy, Goldberger, and Tarule, 1986). We know that, once inside a walled or virtual classroom, many female students may experience (1) professors untrained in effective teaching (even one who has no knowledge of research into gender-related differences in learning styles or who is unaware that many assumed truths are in fact socially constructed and reflect gender biases in their original research), (2) "report talk" rather than "rapport talk" (Tannen, 1990), or competitive and male-dominated discussions, (3) appropriation, not recognition, of knowledge (e.g., male promotion of collaborative learning as if they invented it), (4) isolation more than serious intellectual involvement, (5) gender-based stereotyping, and (6) applications of rules and rights rather than development of relationships.

We can expect that, when helping many women to make a successful comeback into higher education and develop learning-to-learn skills, we have to focus less on the three "R's" of receive, retain, and return, and more on respect, re-frame and re-apply, so that relevant knowledge is generated and used.

Barriers

A canon of distance education is *access*. Women's barriers to education have been documented with depressing regularity (e.g., Evans, 1995; Grace, 1991; Lunneborg, 1994). Margaret Grace summarizes many of the barriers in terms of "disjunctions between the experiential realities of women and girls, and the requirements of distance-education institutions" (p. 71). Patricia Lunneborg (1994) uses the stories of 14 English women to illustrate how situational, institutional, contextual, and psychosocial difficulties operate in a very complex mix and with not always happy results. Chère Campbell Gibson's (1996) study of mostly female bachelor's degree students underscores key psychological barriers relevant to the development of helpful academic self-concepts; a feminist theory analysis could now make even more sense of the findings. Karen Evans (Evans, 1995, p. 12) took a wide view of barriers for her study and categorized them as formal entry requirements, domestication of women's labour, financial dependency/poverty, traditional curricula, and instrumental pedagogies.

Grace points to another kind of barrier, but one that also affects female distance educators. It is an alienation that I and some other female colleagues feel regarding learning designs and technology. We feel isolated when many of the discussion agendas and applications of new technologies are set by others; what is considered 'good' (usually by males) is assumed to be 'good' for me. I have been sent advertising that tells me how a new computer will help me be an effective "warrior" in today's competitive environments; I've somewhat patronizingly been told on occasion how new technologies will dazzle my field of practice. These folks never ask me how I teach, and rarely admit how poor human dynamics or an inappropriate learning design will undermine the use of any technology. The following lament expressed by Jackie Cook in 1989 is uncomfortably relevant today:

> Why am I confronted by bureaucratic history and brochures of electronic whizzery? Why is that most problematic of issues, the teacher/student relationship, addressed in the main by [a telephone company]? (Grace, 1991, p. 58).

Technology

Appropriate technology application is one of the major issues in contemporary distance education. You may regard it as a David and Goliath fight between the small forces of critical assessment and the huge forces of commerce and innovation. Or you may see it as either a seduction in progress or a pre-nuptial agreement under negotiation. Or you may expect that utopian views about technology will be overtaken by dystopian views. Regardless, we cannot escape the recognition that the shaping and use of any technology reflects the influences of societal assumptions, values, and dynamics, especially regarding the use of public and private power and the generation of wealth (Kenway, 1997; Menzies, 1996).

Technology here refers to a brace of conferencing technologies — audio, audiographics, video, and computer. They share the capacity for two-way, many-to-many discussion, either in synchronous or asynchronous time.

Until the early 1980s, distance education dialogue was a one-to-one, paper-based process between learner and teacher; it was often very successful, but lacking the current attractions of real-time and learner-to-learner communications mediated by new technology. Now learners and teachers can theoretically use telephones and computers to create high-speed, high-volume, two-way communications. But there's a catch.

If we are serious about bringing more women into effective distance learning modes, we have to confront two sets of dynamics. First, many women regard technology as a tool, not something to fall in love with (Spender, 1995). They don't have the time or inclination to spend hours trying to conquer the finer points of a software program. Second, many women have to confront gender-based stereotypes about their attitude toward and skills in computer technology and negative experiences once they use the technology (Taylor, Kramarae, and Ebben, 1993).

Earlier research has shown these effects in such technologies as the telephone, architecture, and domestic appliances (Cockburn and Ormrod, 1993; Kramarae, 1988; Rakow, 1992; Weisman, 1992). Technology use is governed by many factors associated with gender-related societal expectations and resource inequities — in the home as well as in public places. Rakow's (1992) summary of her research into women's use of the telephone, for example, reinforces current discussions about the Internet:

> Though the telephone has the technical capacity to level social hierarchies, to end feelings of isolation and loneliness, ... technical possibility has not translated into social practice. ... [The telephone] has become a site at which gender relations are organized, experienced, and accomplished in both the family and the larger community and political world . (p. 154)

Other writers express similar concerns about the women's limited perceptions of their technological attitudes and skill sets, and situate their thinking in factors seen in wider societal context (e.g., Akman, 1996; Busch, 1995; Kramarae and Kramer, 1995; Shashaani, 1994; Spender, 1995; Wajcman, 1991):

> The ideological impetus behind technological development, women's relative poverty to men, women's exclusion from the technological realm throughout our history, and "women's computational reticence" caused by technology's anchoring in values most often associated with men may all contribute to a particular and unique juncture between women and technology. (Akman, 1996, p. 24)

Women researchers advise that uncritical use of technologies will result in further exclusion of women from educational participation (e.g., Kenway, 1997; Kirkup and von Prümmer, 1997; Menzies, 1996; O'Rourke and Schachter, 1997). Heather Menzies argues that "If we're not careful, the new digital networks could become not the 'extensions of women' but the 'contractions' of women" (1997, p. 2). Ursula Franklin (1997)uses half a century of research experience with various technologies and critical analyses of their social impacts to argue for a sense of balance when we engage with any technology:

> Be mindful of how the tool shapes the task. And that you only find this out when you learn about the tool. Learn what is in this Internet. But then keep your head clear and go back to your goals. ... When is that moment when the intangibles of the potluck far outweigh the elegance of a message on the Internet? (pp. 11-12)

Another, and more alarming aspect of the Internet, cannot be ignored because it has such an impact upon the sense of 'safe place' so needed by many female learners. Psychological safety counts for many reasons, not the least being the need for intellectual space and interpersonal support while a learner is going through significant changes in how and why she thinks as she does. Outright intimidation or 'hacking' into a course 'place' in an environment of reduced communication cues becomes easy, as current stories of online interpersonal problems attest. Hear Franklin (1997) again on this point:

> You are also in a public medium, and you are flagged and visible. The Internet ...is one of the most infiltrated and infiltratable highways in the world. (p. 10)

It is reassuring to note that women can claim places in the use of technologies to enhance their access to education. For example, the United States had Anna Ticknor establishing a successful correspondence study system at the end of the nineteenth century. In Canada, at mid-twentieth century, Isabel Wilson of the Canadian Association for Adult Education wrote hundreds of well-balanced study guides for use by rural and urban discussion groups linked into Canadian Broadcasting Company national radio broadcasts. These were designed to help folks get together to analyze "hot" issues of the day and feed back their results for distribution across the country. The kitchen table, the radio, and the print materials were the sustaining technologies. Later in Canada, we saw the establishment of CJRT Open College in Toronto, the only radio station of its kind in North America; May Maskow Ras followed Margaret Norquay as its director.

Increasing numbers of women who can afford access to the Internet are developing extensive networks and guidelines for use. Canadian examples include the extensive Women'space Network out of Nova Scotia (*Women'space*), practical manuals (Balka, 1997; Burge and Roberts, 1998), and research into complex policy issues around access, costs, institutional adoption issues, and government regulatory issues (Keough, 1997; Menzies, 1996; O'Rourke and Schachter, 1997; Shade, 1997).

Guidelines

All in all, technology, barriers, curricula, and participation factors are key ingredients in a complicated recipe for effective women's learning in distance-modes.

Yet, if the gender-based issues in distance education are complex, it does not necessarily follow that guidelines for effective practice have to be long and convoluted. They can be succinct, with unnerving simplicity.

These guidelines arise for me from two assumptions. First, that the two basic adult motivating drives to action — a sense of personal autonomy and competence, and a sense of belonging or personal connectedness — apply to females as much as to males (MacKeracher, 1996) but that how these dynamics play out often involves gender-related processes. A consequent guideline for a teacher can then be phrased as a question: "What is happening now in the classroom that is hindering competence and connectedness?" In other words, worry more about how educational settings de-motivate learners, because we cannot 'motivate' any learner — that is an internal process. Second, that any guideline is limited until one understands how the issues operate in specific contexts. This task is a real challenge because it involves in part looking for the covert as well as the overt dynamics.

Hear an experienced female educator state her four basic guidelines:

> A vital component of initial contact from the instructor must be a strong dose of TLC (tender loving care). It is essential that early in the process, the learners be confirmed in the decisions they have made to enter the course, that their position as "knowers" be strengthened, and that their life-experiences be acknowledged as valuable steps in the learning process (Laidlaw, 1997).

My guidelines have three parts — constructivist, woman-friendly, and technology. The constructivist and woman-friendly guidelines focus on how a learner takes responsibility for knowledge construction, with faculty guidance, of course. They are not easy strategies to implement: many learners in my experience are habituated into being passive, uncritical recipients of others' knowledge; and many faculty mistakenly think that such a teaching model reduces their importance in the learning process (it does change their roles). The technology guidelines address the task of technology application, maintenance, and the divisions between the techno-rich and the techno-poor.

Constructivist Guidelines

- Learning resources and learning tasks are relevant to the learner's real-world contexts. Authenticity is seen in the complex, often ambiguous problems and ideas to work on, and in the use of the learner's personal practical knowledge.

- Learner is encouraged to set goals and activities, under guidance and with due standards.

- Learner is helped to challenge current mental frameworks and examine value systems.

- Errors and hesitancies are used as natural components of the learning process.

- Talking aloud in order to think is as valued as writing to express end-products of learning.

- Make no assumptions about any woman.

- Recursive travels through a set of ideas or skills will enhance the development of expert knowing.

- Watching a skilled person think through a problem can help a less-skilled learner work efficiently.

- Time is needed and given for in-depth thinking, for re-visiting topics, for checking out tentative ideas.

- Learners explain how they know something, how they reached a conclusion or refined a new skill, for example.

- The dynamics as well as the components in learning are surfaced as much as possible, to help meta-cognitive development.

- A learner's feeling of insecurity or doubt are legitimized, not dismissed by faculty. Use the first signs of a cognitive stumble or an emotional difficulty as evidence of the 'work' of learning.

- Encourage multiple ways to represent knowledge-under-construction; e.g., metaphorical and intuitive thought, visual mapping of concept development.

Women-Friendly Guidelines

Woman-friendly guidelines attend to gender-related but not necessarily gender-specific factors (Eichles, 1988) that may affect learning. The factors include social power differences, self-worth, and self-confidence, epistemological practice, and general academic competence. Here is my basic set of guidelines:

- Acknowledge the sheer diversity among women in terms of life experience.

- Watch for signals of impatience or worse as women confront a new technology or recognize the impacts of societal constructions of life roles.

- Do not tolerate the use of language or research that shows gender bias or unwarranted gender-exclusivity.

- Watch for male domination of discussion and other forms of typically male styles of interaction.

- Expect that at-home study conditions may include a struggle to reach the family computer or study at times when other family members are watching TV.

- Look out for self-denigration during class discussions and/or dysfunctionally high and self-imposed academic standards.

- Tactfully refuse to do the learner's thinking for her, but support her through the pains of self-growth.

- Don't set class schedules during times of day when child-care may be a problem.

- Use and look for the knowledge that women learners value and express.

- Encourage critical epistemological assessments of presumed 'truths.'

- Help all learners — male and female — talk with, not past, each other.

- Accept that many women will adopt critical and practical approaches to technology use.

- Watch for appropriations of knowledge without due recognition.

- Suggest that a less-than-perfectly run house is OK, indeed expected.

Technology Guidelines

The technology-related guidelines focus on access and use issues, as we change from a POTS (plain old telephone service) to a PANS (public access network service) scenario (Shade, 1997).

One obvious guideline is to boldly interrogate each technology. Ask why and how may it be useful, which older technologies may do the job better or at a lesser cost, and what on-going operational costs will be evident. Ask who most stands to benefit by the introduction of new and high technology and what kinds of intellectual and ergonomic skills are required to make the best use of human interactions via the technology.

I have learned over the years that technical operational skills are usually the least of the teacher's worries — the biggest challenge comes from facilitating the cognitive operations of the learners! It takes some bravery to carry out such interrogations. We should be thankful that learners don't sue for cognitive malpractice!

The following guidelines are taken from the latest Canadian treatment of this issue (O'Rourke and Schachter, 1997):

- Observe and keep track of developments.

- Keep a history.

- Consider appropriate risk assessment strategies.

- Maintain a "reality check" file.

- Keep track of what works well and what doesn't.
- Champion good examples and analyze the bad examples.
- Identify decision points.
- Discover what the options really are.
- Explore underlying values and question the values behind the statements.
- Check definitions of terminology.
- Examine the access and equity of new initiatives.
- Ask funders and decision-makers about policies regarding equity provisions.
- Develop a comprehensive definition of "equity of access."

They look so obvious and so simple, don't they?

I must end this chapter, knowing that I have only touched the surface of a challenging but inescapable issue in contemporary distance education. Gender-related differences in how adults learn cannot be dismissed as indulgences of privileged academics. They require sustained attention, knowing that 'distance' raises psychological barriers to programs and course completions as well as geographical and fiscal barriers.

Female distance educators have come a long way since the early 1980s in drawing attention to the issues; now the efforts continue in the gendered worlds of the new technologies. If we don't get those identity and inclusion issues right this time, we will have lost a huge opportunity — in terms of human potential as well as of economic benefits.

References

Akman, J. (1996). Increasing women's use of electronic networks: The women's networking and support program of the Association for Progressive Communications. *Feminist Collections*, 17(2), 24-26.

Balka, E. (1997). *Computer networking: Spinsters on the web.* Ottawa: Canadian Research Institute for the Advancement of Women.

Belenky, M. F., Clinchy, B.M., Goldberger, N.R., and Tarule, J.M. (1986). *Women's ways of knowing: The development of self, voice and mind.* New York: Basic Books.

Bryson M., & de Castell, M. (1995). So we've got a chip on our shoulder! Sexing the texts of "educational technology." In J. Gaskell & J. Willinsky (Eds.), *Gender in/forms curriculum: From enrichment to transformation* (pp. 21-42). New York: Teachers College Press.

Burge, E.J. (1996). Inside-out thinking about distance teaching: Making sense of reflective practice. *Journal of the American Society for Information Science,* 47(11), 843-848.

Burge, E.J. (1990). Women as learners: Issues for visual and virtual classroom. *The Canadian Journal for the Study of Adult Education,* 4 (2), 1-24.

Burge, E.J., & Carter, N.M. (1997, June). It's building but is it designing? Constructing a web-based learning environment. Paper for the 1997 World Conference of the International Council for Distance Education, Pennsylvania State University.

Burge, E., & Lensjky, H. (1990). Women studying in distance education: Issues and principles. *Journal of Distance Education,*5(2), 20-37.

Burge, E.J., & Roberts, J.M. (1998). *Classrooms with a differrence.* Montreal: McGraw-Hill.

Busch, T. (1995). Gender differences in self-efficacy and attitudes toward computers. *Journal of Educational Computing Research,* 12 (2), 147-158.

Coates, M. (1994). *Women's education. Buckingham, UK: SRHE/Open Uni - versity Press.*

Cockburn, C., & Ormrod, C. (1993). *Gender and technology in the making.* London: Sage.

Eichler, M. (1988). *Nonsexist research methods: A practical guide.* Boston, MA: Allyn & Bacon.

Evans, K. (1995, November). Barriers to participation of women in technological education and the role of distance education. Occasional paper No. 1. Vancouver, BC: The Commonwealth of Learning. Unpublished manuscript.

Faith, K. (Ed.). (1988). *Toward new horizons for women in distance educa - tion: International perspectives.* London: Routledge.

Fosnot, C. W. (Ed.). (1996). *Constructivism: Theory, perspectives, and practice.* New York: Teachers College Press.

Franklin, U. (1997). *Every tool shapes the task: Communities and the information highway.* Vancouver, BC: Lazara Press.

Gabriel, S., & Smithson, I. (Eds.). (1990). *Gender in the classroom: Power and pedagogy.* Urbana: University of Illinois Press.

Gaskell, J., & Willinsky, J. (Eds.). (1995). *Gender in/forms curriculum: From enrichment to transformation.* New York: Teachers College Press.

Gibson, C. Campbell. (1996). Towards an understanding of academic self-concept in distance education. *The American Journal of Distance Education,* 10(1), 23-36.

Gilligan, C. (1982). *In a different voice: Psychological theory and women's development.* Cambridge, MA: Harvard University Press.

Goldberger, N.R., Tarule, J.M., Clinchy, B.M.,&Belenky, M.F. (Eds.). (1996). *Knowledge, difference, and power: Essays inspired by women's ways of knowing.* New York: BasicBooks.

Grace, M. (1991). Gender issues in distance education. In T. Evans & B. King (Eds.), *Beyond the text: Contemporary writings in distance education* (pp.56-74). Geelong, Victoria, Australia: Deakin University Press.

Johnson, K. (1988). Convocation speech, Athabasca University, Alberta, Canada. Unpublished manuscript.

Kenway, J. (1997). Backlash in cyberspace: Why "girls need modems." In L. G. Roman & L. Eyre (Eds.), *Dangerous territories: Struggles for difference and equality in education* (pp. 255-274). London: Routledge.

Keough, E.M (1997). Distance education: Thoughts on current policy directions and their impacts. *Communique,* 3/4, 3-7.

Kirkup, G. (1988). Sowing seeds: Initiatives for improving the representation of women. In K. Faith (Ed.), *Toward new horizons for women in distance education: International perspectives* (pp. 287-312). London: Routledge.

Kirkup, G. (1996). The importance of gender. In R. Mills & A. Tait (Eds.) *Supporting the learner in open and distance learning* (pp. 146-164). London: Pitman.

Kirkup, G., & von Prümmer, C. (1990). Support and connectedness: The needs of women distance education students. *Journal of Distance Education,* 5(2), 9-31.

Kirkup, G., & von Prümmer, C. (1997). Distance education for European women. *The European Journal of Women's Studies,* 4(1), 39-62.

Kramarae, C. (Ed.) (1988). *Technology and women's voices: Keeping in touch*. London: Routledge & Kegan Paul.

Kramarae, C., & Kramer, J. (1995). Legal snarls for women in cyberspace. *Internet Research*, 5(2), 14-24.

Laidlaw, S. (1997). Personal communication, February 25.

Lunneborg, P. (1994). *OU women: Undoing educational obstacles*. London: Cassell.

MacKeracher, D. (1996). *Making sense of adult learning*. Toronto: Culture Concepts.

Maher, F. A., & Tetrault, M.K.T. (1994). *The feminist classroom*. New York: BasicBooks.

May, S. (1994). Women's experiences as distance learners: Access and technology. *Journal of Distance Education*, 9(1), 81-98.

Menzies, H. (1996). *Whose brave new world? The information highway and the new economy*. Toronto: Between the Lines.

Menzies, H. (1997, March). Woman-centred learning in the digital universe. Speech delivered in Montreal.

Moran, L. (1990). Inter-institutional collaboration: The case of the Australian inter-university women's studies major. *Journal of Distance Education*, 5(2), 32-48.

Normand, J. (1995). Education of women in Canada. *Canadian Social Trends*, 39, 17-21.

O'Rourke, J., & Schachter, L. (1997). *CCLOW's Janus Project: Promises and prospects of the new learning technologies for adult learning opportunities for women*. Final Report of a discussion paper prepared for the Canadian Congress for Learning Opportunities for Women. Toronto: CCLOW.

Pravda, G. (1994). Women-friendly approaches to teaching and learning:An overview of selected papers. In M. Coates (Ed.), *Women's education* (pp.154-159). Buckingham,UK: SRHE/Open University Press.

Rakow, L.F. (1992). *Gender on the line: Women, the telephone, and community life*. Urbana: University of Illinois Press.

Shade, L.R. (1997). Using a gender-based analysis in developing a Canadian access strategy: Backgrounder report. Unpublished paper for the Ad Hoc Committee for the Workshop on Access to the Information Highway. Toronto: University of Toronto, Faculty of Information Studies.

Shashaani, L. (1994). Gender differences in computer experience and its influence on computer attitudes. *Journal of Educational Computing Research*, 11 (4),347-367.

Smith, E., & Norlen, V.S. (1994). Tele-distance education in women's studies: Issues for feminist pedagogy. *The Canadian Journal for the Study of Adult Education*, 8 (2), 29-43.

Spender, D. (1996). *Nattering on the Net: Women, power and cyberspace*. Toronto: Garamond Press.

Spronk, B. (1994). Gender in distance education. *Open Praxis*, 1, 10-11.

Tannen, D. (1990). *You just don't understand: Women and men in conversation*. New York: Ballentine.

Taylor, H.J., Kramarae, C., & Ebben, M. (Eds). (1993). *Women, information, technology and scholarship*. Urbana: University of Illinois, Center for Advanced Study.

Taylor, L., & Kirkup, G. (1994). From the local to the global. *Open Praxis*, 1, 12-14.

Umeå Universitet (1993, June). *Feminist pedagogy and women-friendly perspectives in distance education*. Papers presented at the International WIN Working Conference, 10-13 June, Umea, Sweden.

von Prümmer, C. (1993). Women in distance education: A researcher's view. In *Research in distance education: Present situation and forecasts* . Report from a Nordic Conference in Umea (pp. 51-67). Umeå, Sweden: Umeå Universitet.

von Prümmer, C. (1997). Distance education as a second chance for women. Paper for the 1997 World Conference of the International Council for Distance Education.

Wajcman, J. (1991). *Feminism confronts technology*. University Park, PA: The Pennsylvania State University Press.

Weisman, L. K. (1992). *Discrimination by design: A feminist critique of the man-made environment*. Urbana: University of Illinois Press.

Wilson, B. G. (1995). *Constructivist learning environments.*Englewood Cliffs, NJ: Educational Technology Publications.

Women'space magazine. Available from Women'space, RR#1, Scotsburn, Nova Scotia, Canada. B0K 1R0

Chapter 3

Understanding and supporting the culturally diverse distance learner

Irene Sanchez and Charlotte N. Gunawardena

This chapter focuses on culturally diverse distance learners and examines ways in which the needs of these learners can be taken into consideration in the design of distance instruction and learner support. We begin with a discussion of changing demographics in the United States and the educational needs of adults from different cultures, analyses of the literature on individual differences and learning styles, and the influence of culture on learning. A learning style profile of Hispanic adult learners will be discussed as a case example showing how the understanding of the Hispanic learner as described in the profile can be applied to the design of distance instruction and learner support systems.

The Growing Cultural Diversity of Learners

The United States has been home to many people with diverse cultural and ethnic backgrounds for centuries; however, there is little doubt that the face of America is changing. Recent articles in popular magazines such as *Time* and *Newsweek* have chronicled the change in America's population or what they call the "Browning of America," and the increase in numbers of ethnic minority populations in many parts of the country. Rodriguez (1988) has noted that by the year 2000, the "current minority will have become the majority" in the 53 most-populated cities in the country. The increase in ethnic minority populations is having an impact in two major American institutions, namely the work force and the educational system.

One of the major work force-related trends that is often cited is the magnitude of cultural diversity that will characterize the work forces of organizations beginning in the 1990s (Cox, 1993). Gardenswartz and Rowe (1993) cite five changes in demographics that will impact the work force. The changes are fundamental and far-reaching. How American organizations deal with the dilemmas presented by these trends will affect not only their success but also their approach to promoting learning in the organization. The education and training of the work force of the future is also affected. These changes are:

- *Increase in the number of women in the work force.* By the year 2000, women will make up almost half (47%) of the labor force and 60% of new job entrants into the work force (Hudson Institute, 1988).

- *Increase in the number of minorities in the work force.* The Hudson Institute Report predicts that as early as the year 2000, minorities will make up 29% of the work force. This increase is particularly true for Hispanics, whose population has increased by 30% since 1980 and is increasing at a rate five times greater than other groups, making them the fastest growing group in the U.S. The Census Bureau estimates that their population will reach 29 million by the year 2000 and that, by the year 2050, Hispanics will constitute 30% of the population and may become the largest minority group in the country (Valdivieso and Davis, 1988).

- *Increase in number of immigrants.* Today's newcomers are not primarily European, as they were in the early 1900s; most are coming from Latin America, Asia, and the Middle East. These new immigrants are not as willing to assimilate and give up their unique cultures (Hodgkinson, 1985).

- *The aging of the work force.* The demographic bulge created by the baby boom as it passes into maturity moves a large proportion of the work force into middle age. While the majority of workers in the next decade will still be in their most productive years (30-54), the labor force is slowly getting older.

- *Rise in education and skill requirement for employment.* Jobs in the 21st century will require a more highly skilled work force in a society where education and skill levels are declining. Work force 2000 predicts that the majority of jobs from now on will require education beyond high school, signaling the need for bold new methods of training employees in both basic and job-related skills.

These demographic changes will impact workplace training and require a response that includes increased need and opportunities for distance education.

The increase in both ethnic minority populations and cultural diversity will also impact the educational arena. By the year 2010, minority populations will be majority populations in certain segments of the county (Hodgkinson, 1985). Ross-Gordon (1991) points out that in 25 of the largest school districts in the country, the student population is composed of a "minority" majority and that 26% of all students in the country come from a minority group. Sanders and Wiserman (1990) point out that classroom demography is becoming increasingly multicultural, thereby creating a critical need to pay attention to the diverse learning styles associated with various ethnic groups.

Distance learners in many education and training programs now and in the future will be composed of different cultural groups. But there will be other related differences that emerge across diverse groups of learners that need to be carefully considered as educators design and deliver distance education.

Individual Differences and Learning Styles

During the past twenty years, there has been increasing interest in educational research focusing on individual differences. One of those individual differences has been learning styles, defined as "people's characteristic way of information processing, feeling and behaving in and toward learning situations" (Smith, 1986, p. 24).

The assessment of learning styles and the impact of matching learning style and teaching style has been the focus of many studies. Dunn et. al.

(1981) report that the learning styles research in the past decade has "yielded useful findings about the effects of environmental sociological and cognitive preferences on the achievement of students." (p. 50) "Further, many researchers have specifically analyzed how culturally different students begin to concentrate, process and retain new and different academic information" (Dunn, 1983, p. 25). Reviewing the results of these studies, Dunn continues noting that in all groups of learners — gifted, average or high achievers — there were statistically significant differences among and between groups of culturally different students. Although each ethnic and racial group may exhibit statistically significant differences with clusters of specific learning style variables, each group also contained individuals with widely diverse learning styles.

The history of learning styles research can be summarized as a result of work conducted by a group of psychologists in America, namely the Fells Institute Group (Kagan and colleagues), the Menninger Foundation group (Klein, Gardner, Schesinger, and Holzman), the Brooklyn group (Witkin and colleagues), and a group from Europe and Australia: Marton, Pask, Saljo, and Entwistle (Bonham, 1988). Curry (1987) describes the chief difference in their work as the fact that North American research was based upon cognitive psychology and included "psychometric considerations" as an integral part of the research and classified learning behaviors as strategies that were subject to change, whereas the European/Australian group focused upon detailed learning behaviors based on small numbers of learners and focused more on deeper "style" concepts.

Out of this research, numerous theories of cognitive processing and controls were developed. The most notable include theories of cognitive control, cognitive flexibility, and cognitive strategies employed by learners in the learning process. The following description presents the key focus and theorist of the major theories:

Cognitive Control Theories

Field-dependence vs. Field-independence: Witkin (1977) and his colleagues studied how individuals orient themselves in space and analyzed the relationship between an individual's visual and kinesthetic cues and the degree of emphasis an individual places on internal (self) or external (field) referents. He designated the tendency to rely primarily on "internal referents" as being field-independent and the tendency to systematically rely upon "external referents" as being field-dependent. He posited that the internal frames of reference available to field-independent people allowed them to structure situations on their own and therefore, as learners, they are internally motivated, prefer to learn on their own, arrive at their own learning strategies, and prefer intrinsic rewards. Field-dependents, on the other hand, are holistic, global learners who prefer instructor guidance and involvement, are externally motivated, and prefer group work and extrinsic rewards.

Global vs. Analytical: The two researchers primarily identified with this theory are Kirby (1988) and Schmeck (1988). The characteristics assigned to global learners include being field-dependent, formulation of global impressions rather than precisely articulated codes, random and numerous associations, intuitive thinkers, consider feelings in making decisions, less emphasis on control, impulsive, holistic, and gifted at seeing similarities in situations. Analytical learners are described as being field-independent, having focused attention, focus on and remember details, interested in how things operate, emphasis on the proper way of doing things, prefer step-by-step, sequential, organized schemes, exhibit controlled thinking divorced from feelings, gifted at logical thinking, can see differences rather than similarities, and prefer sequential, serial learning activities.

Cognitive Flexibility Theories

Constricted vs. Flexible Control: This theory developed by Menninger Foundation group (Gardner, Holzman, Klein, Linton, and Spence, 1959) analyzes the ability to focus on relevant stimuli by ignoring distractions, and the ability to inhibit incorrect verbal response (Jonassen and Grabowski, 1993). It is also a measure of an individual's flexibility or readiness to change his or her judgment of a proposed solution to a problem. The flexible individual is not as easily distracted by conflicting cues as a constricted processor and therefore is better able to restrict irrelevant responses.

Impulsivity vs. Reflectivity: Kagan (1966) and his colleagues proposed this bipolar construct, which is sometimes known as cognitive tempo. It measures the individual's ability to reflect on the accuracy of an answer and to inhibit responding impulsively. Individuals at the reflective end have longer response times and commit fewer errors than impulsive individuals, who answer quickly and with greater frequency of error leading to the belief that reflectives think before they act. Kagan (1966) proposed that cognitive tempo is developmental in nature and that individuals become more reflective as they age.

Focal Attention/Scanning vs. Focusing: This theory (Santostefano, 1964) describes the differences in the processing of stimulus fields and measures the individual's ability to scan a field and cognitively record and compare visual and verbal properties from available information. It measures the intensity (active or passive) and extensiveness (narrow or broad) of scanning.

Cognitive Strategies

Holist vs. Serialist: Pask (1988) describes holist learners as paying attention to global aspects of the learning situation and serialist as paying attention to detailed, sequential analysis of the learning elements. His learners closely parallel the concept of global and analytical learners.

Right-Brained vs. Left-Brained: Torrence and Rockenstein's (1988) theory is associated with creativity or problem-solving strategies used in learning situations. They describe left-brained thinkers as conforming individuals who prefer structure and verbal material in order to look for specific facts to sequence into ideas and draw conclusions to solve problems logically to improve things. Right-brained thinkers are non-conforming persons who prefer open-ended assignments, exploration, and imagery and who look for main ideas to show relationships in order to produce new ideas or invent something new.

Visual vs. Haptic: Associated with the work of Lownefield (1946), Kagan (1965), and Galbraith and James (1985), this theory describes an individual's preference for processing information with visual or haptic orientations. According to Jonassen and Grabowski (1993), visually oriented individuals use spatial relations, visual discrimination, figure-ground discrimination, and object recognition to gather information, whereas the haptic individuals prefer to extract information using tactile and kinesthetic manipulation of objects.

Visual vs. Verbalizer: This cognitive style describes the individual's preference for attending to and processing verbal or visual information. It is associated with the work of Paivio (1971), Richardson (1977), and Swassing and Barbe (1979), who describe verbalizers as preferring to process information from words, spoken or written, and visualizers as preferring pictures, charts, and imagery to obtain information.

Leveling vs. Sharpening: This cognitive style measures how individuals perceive and memorize images. Levelers tend to condense story elements, simplify stories, frequently miss changes or inconsistencies, merge new impressions and experience with older ones, and integrate information more readily into memory. Sharpeners, on the other hand, are able to clearly differentiate between discrete images and identify the small differences between them, recall structure, and remember details, and they rely more on rote memory than levelers.

Knowing these theories and understanding the impact of individual differences is important to the distance educator in designing instruction as well as recognizing that differences exist not only between cultural groups but also within these groups.

Influences of Culture on Learning

Guild (1994) reminds educators of the connection between culture and learning style and that effective educational practices stem from an understanding of the way that individuals learn, including knowing the students' culture and its effect upon learning. As Anderson (1988) notes,

> All components of a culture are built upon some basic conceptual system or philosophical world view, and the various cultural systems tend to include the same general themes (life, death, birth, mortality, human nature, religion, etc.). Even though these beliefs appear across cultures, they can be viewed differently within each culture. (p. 3)

Anderson (1988, p. 6) suggests that those in the dominant Western world view include Euro-Americans (primarily males) and minorities with a high degree of acculturation. Many Euro-American females and the vast majority of other cultural groups in the U.S. would be categorized as sharing a Non-Western world view. The fundamental dimensions of Non-Western and Western world views and those who share aspects of that world view are seen in Table 1.

Based on an extensive review of the literature, Anderson further posits cognitive style and cultural groupings comparisons as seen in Table 2 (Anderson, 1988, p. 6). While reminding the reader that no one style is better than any other, he does note that Euro-American style, characterized by field-independence and analytic thinking with limited affective thinking, is often most valued in our higher education settings.

Anderson (1988, p. 8) concludes that these differences must be accounted for in the educational setting and states that "a different set of understandings about the way diverse populations communicate, behave, and think needs to be developed by educators. Until this occurs, education

Non-Western	Western
Emphasize group cooperation	Emphasize individual competition
Achievement as it reflects group	Achievement for the individual
Value harmony with nature	Must master and control nature
Time is relative	Adhere to rigid time schedule
Accept affective expression	Limit affective expression
Extended family	Nuclear family
Holistic thinking	Dualistic thinking
Religion permeates culture	Religion is distinct from other parts of culture
Accept world views of other cultures	Feel their world view is superior
Socially oriented	Task-oriented

Table 1: Some Fundamental Dimensions
of Non-Westerrn vs. Western World Views

will continue to stagnate in the dark ages and educators will provide lip service rather than action to the egalitarian values associated with pluralism and multiculturalism .... As professional educators we must settle for nothing less."

Dunn and Griggs (1995) note that each cultural group also tends to have some learning style elements that distinguish it from other cultural groups. However, they point out that a consistent finding in research is that each individual within a family, classroom, or culture has unique learning style preferences that differ from those of their siblings, parents, peers, and cultural group. They state that instructors need to be aware of three critical factors:

• Universal principles of learning do exist.

• Culture influences both the learning process and its outcomes.

• Each individual has unique learning style preferences that affect his or her potential for achievement.

Dunn and Griggs (1995) observe that cultural values influence the socialization practices of all ethnic groups, which in turn affect how individuals prefer to learn. However, focusing on their specific research,

Field-Dependent	Field-Independent
Relational/Holistic	Analytic
Affective	Non-Affective

Characteristics	**Characteristics**
1. Perceive elements as a part of a total picture	1. Perceive elements as discrete from their background.
2. Do best on verbal tasks.	2. Do best on analytic tasks.
3. Learn material which has a human social content and which is characterized by fantasy and humor.	3. Learn material that is inanimate and impersonal more easily.
4. Performance influenced by authorizing figure's expression of conficence or doubt.	4. Peformance not greatly affected by the oopinions of others.
5. Style conflicts with traditional school environment.	5. Style matches up with most school environments.

Table 2: Cognitive Style Comparison

which studied learning styles of Native American adolescents, they note that the learning differences within the Native American population are greater than the mean differences between Native Americans and other ethnic groups, echoing Dunn's 1983 caution. Thus, when teaching Native American adolescents, it is important to understand the group cultural heritage and values. However, it is also important to keep in mind that, within groups, individuals differ significantly from each other, and therefore, it is equally important to identify and respond to the individual's learning style preferences.

One additional point does need to be considered. While matching teaching and learning styles may yield higher achievement, providing learners with activities that require them to broaden their repertoire of learning styles more fully prepares them to function in our diverse society. There is a need to provide a delicate balance of activities that provide opportunities to learn in preferred ways and activities that challenge the learner to learn in new or less preferred ways. For example, combining competitive and collaborative work encourages learners to develop skills in both modes of learning, better preparing them to function in the world of work and family.

A Case Study — Hispanic Adult Learners

In order to understand how culture affects learning, Sanchez (1996) studied the learning style preferences of one group of Hispanic adult learners. The study looked at the learning preferences of 240 adult learners, utilizing Curry's (1991) Theoretical Model of Learning Style Components and Effects, and analyzes three essential elements which, combined together, define a learning style:

1. *Motivational maintenance level*, which measures the learner's preference for specific elements in the learning environment and the specific skills of attention, motivation, persistence, and need that the learner brings to the learning situation.

2. *Task engagement level*, which is the interaction between the motivational condition of the learner and the active processing work required by the new learning task and in-cludes such elements as attention, enthusiasm, degree of participation, and concentration exhibited by the learner in the new learning situation.

3. *Cognitive processing level*, which involves the "cognitive information processing habits or controls system" that the learner brings to the learning situation.

The model utilizes three instruments to assess each level. Level One (Motivation Maintenance) is measured by the Friedman and Stritter (1976) *Instructional Preference Questionnaire*, the Grasha and Reichman (1975) *Students Learning Styles Scale*, and the Rezler and Rezmovic (1981) *Learning Preference Inventory*. Level Two (Task Engagement) is assessed using the Kagan (1964) *Matching Familiar Figures Test*, the Schmeck, Ribich, and Ramanaiah (1977) *Inventory of Learning Processes*, and the Weinstein, Palmer, and Schulte (1987) *Learning and Studies Strategies Inventory*. The Third Level (Cognitive Control Functions) meas-ured using the Kolb (1977) *Learning Styles Inventory*, the *Myers-Briggs Type Indicator* (1962), and the Witkin (1971) *Group Embedded Figures Test*.

The 240 subjects completed the nine instruments using, a Greco-Latin Square design to control for "test fatigue." Subjects completed the two timed tests *(Matching Familiar Figures Test* and *Group Embedded Figures Test)* in one session and then were given the seven other instruments to complete on their own. Data was analyzed using measures of central tendency, t-tests, chi-square, and factor analysis. The results of the data were utilized in developing a profile of learning preferences for each of the scales measured by the nine instruments. Demographic factors such as gender, degree of bilingualism, educational level, and age were examined to assess their impact upon the scales. A sub-sample of subjects (n=24) were interviewed to assess whether they felt their individual learning styles profile accurately reflected or matched their conceptions of how they learn and to further validate the acceptability of the nine instruments for use with Hispanic adult learners.

Learning Styles Preferences for Hispanic Adult Learners

The following profile of learning style preferences for the study population emerged. This profile describes learning preferences for Hispanic adult learners for the various scales of the instruments and the three levels of Curry's (1991) model. The list of preferences that follow were significant. These scales (variables) received the highest scores and can be interpreted as strong preferences for the variable or as a strong propensity to utilize the component represented by the scale as a learning strategy.

Motivation maintenance findings show the study group displayed a high preference for:

- Feedback — degree to which students find evaluative mechanisms such as tests helpful in learning

- Participation over avoidance — desire to participate rather than not to participate in classroom activities

- Collaborative over competitive — preference to share ideas and work in groups over a desire to perform better than others in class and to compete with other students for teachers' attention and grades

- Concrete over abstract — preference for tangible, specific, practical tasks over theories, hypotheses, general principles, and concepts

On the task engagement level, learners exhibited the following strong preferences or propensities:

- Fact retention — memory capacity which influences learning

- Elaborative processing — the lengths to which students will go in order to encode new information, such as interrelating new and old information, using visual imagery, rephrasing in one's own words, and thinking of practical applications

- Attitude — attitude and interest in learning in an academic environment

- Motivation — the students' diligence, self-discipline, and willingness to work hard

- Concentration — the students' ability to pay close attention to academic tasks

- Information processing — the use of imagery, verbal elaboration, comprehension-monitoring, and reasoning

- Selecting main idea — the students' ability to pick out important information

- Test strategies — the students' approach to preparing for and taking examinations

- Reflectivity — the measure of cognitive tempo or ability to reflect on the accuracy of the available hypotheses

In terms of the cognitive controls level, the Hispanic learners in this study preferred:

- Active experimentation — an action-based, active approach to learning

- Judgment over perception — the preference for using a judgment process (thinking or feeling) rather than a perceptive process (sensing or intuitive) for dealing with the outer world

Being aware of these preferences may be useful in designing instructional programs for this group or a similar group of Hispanics. It is also important to keep in mind that these components were affected by the demographic variables of gender, educational level, degree of bilingualism, and age; therefore, these elements must also be taken into account when designing instruction for this group.

It is imperative to remember that these results cannot be generalized to all Hispanics. As Guild (1994) points out, "Generalizations about a *group* of people often lead to naive inference about *individual* members of that group" (p. 20). Further, Cox, and Rameriz (1981) caution that misusing information about the learning preferences of a group can lead to stereotyping and labeling rather than the identification of educationally meaningful differences among individuals.

If a distance education course were designed that would support culturally diverse learners who displayed these characteristics, the following ideas might be taken into consideration.

Implications for Designing Distance Instruction and Learner Support

Based on the learning style profile for Hispanic learners described in the Sanchez (1996) study, it is possible to provide guidelines for designing distance instruction and support for these learners. In general, it can be stated that distance instructors must employ a variety of teaching strategies to accommodate a variety of learning style preferences. While it is possible to use a variety of teaching strategies — group work, lecture, discussion, role play — through a single medium, such as audio teleconferencing, it is also important to consider employing a variety of media, capitalizing on the unique strengths of each medium. In general, when trying to accommodate a variety of learning styles in the instructional design, it is always best to design alternative activities to reach the same objective and give the students the option of selecting from these alternative activities those which best meet their preferred learning style.

Reflecting on the maintenance of motivation, the Hispanic learning style profile shows a strong preference for feedback. Faculty teaching at a distance need to be mindful of providing frequent and adequate feedback to support these learners. This can be done through comments on assignments, individual letters, fax, or e-mail. These learners also show a preference for collaborative over competitive activities and like to participate in class activities. Having the opportunity to work in groups on projects that are planned, carried out, and evaluated by the group would accommodate these preferences. An excellent medium for doing this is computer conferencing that supports extended group dialogue. Group activities — such as a discussion on a topic, problem-solving, or role playing — can be planned so that learners can moderate these activities and evaluate themselves. These learners also showed a preference for reflectivity in task engagement and the medium of computer conferencing accommodates reflective learners better than the face-to-face classroom. Where computer conferencing is not available, it is possible to provide for group activities and assignments at remote sites using other means. If there are study centers in the distance education system, then these group activities can be arranged at these centers. If the system of delivery is a satellite-based two-way interactive system or simply audioconferencing, the broadcasts can be broken into segments in which students do group activities and engage in group discussion at their sites. Activities that encourage the application of the concepts taught during the conference to the local environment can be followed by time to report back to the larger class for collaborative learning.

Hispanic learners also showed a preference for concrete over abstract and a preference for active experimentation, that is, a preference for an action-based, active approach to learning. Therefore, teaching strategies should include those that allow learners to plan and carry out projects that require the practical application of principles and theories to real life. It may be useful to design constructive learning environments (Jonassen, 1994) after an introduction to theory and principles, in order to provide learners with an opportunity to share knowledge with others, apply it to real life, test hypotheses, and make meaning for themselves.

The Hispanic adult learners in question also showed a preference for information processing, elaborative processing, and judgment over perception. This implies the ability to engage in higher-order cognitive processing. In order to support these processes, instructors should design activities that engage the learner in processing different types of information, synthesizing information, and making judgments based on that information. Activities using the Internet and the World Wide Web, which offer access to a variety of information, may provide an opportunity for these learners to engage in information processing and elaborative processing. In order to support these activities, novice learners should be first oriented to the technology and then provided with a concept map of the structure of information on the World Wide Web.

These are some of the ways in which the learning style profile for Hispanic adult learners described above can provide guidance for instructional methods, strategies, and support for the distance learner.

Conclusions

The learners in higher education are becoming increasingly diverse. Further, anecdotal reports suggest that the use of instructional technologies that enable teaching and learning at a distance has further diversified higher education by increasing access to a wide variety of cultural groups.

Our challenge is to recognize the diversity of culture and learning styles and to begin to design distance education to enable diverse learners to enhance their learning. The variety of learners, cultures, and learning styles presents a challenge — and variety itself becomes the solution. Providing a variety of instructional activities and resources through a wide array of available instructional technologies gives each learner an opportunity to excel in ways in which he or she prefers to learn. It also serves to challenge learners to expand their repertoire of learning styles, to allow them to more fully function in the diverse world.

References

Anderson, J.A. (1988). Cognitive styles and multicultural populations. *Jour - nal of Teacher Education*, 22, 3-9.

Bennett, C.I. (1990). *Comprehensive multicultural education*, (2nd. Ed.). Needham, MA: Allyn & Bacon.

Bonham, A.L. (1988). Learning styles use: In need to perspective. *Lifelong Learning*, 11, 14-17.

Chute, A.G. (1989). Designing for International Teletraining. Paper published in *International Teleconference Association 1989 Yearbook*, ERIC, ED313 017.

Cox, B., & Rameriz, M. III. (1981). Cognitive styles: Implications for multiethnic education. In J. Banks (Ed.), *Education in the 80's*. Washington, D.C. National Education Association.

Cox, T.H. (1993). *Cultural diversity in organizations: Theory, research and practice*. San Francisco: Berrett-Koehler Publishers, Inc.

Curry, L. (1987). Integrating concepts of cognitive or learning style: a review with attention to psychometric standards. *The Curry Report*. The Learning Styles Network, Center for the Study of Learning and Teaching Styles. Jamaica, New York: St. Johns University.

Curry, L. (1991). Patterns of learning styles across selected medical specialties. *Educational Psychology*, 11, 3(4), 247-277.

Dunn, R. (1983). Learning style and its relationship to exceptionality at both ends of the spectrum. *Exceptional Children*, 4(6), 496-506.

Dunn, R., Dunn, K., & Price, G.E. (1981). *Productivity, environmental preference survey.* Lawrence, KS: Price Systems.

Dunn, R., & Griggs, S.A. (1995). *Multiculturalism and learning style: Teaching and counseling adolescents.* Westport, CT: Praeger.

Dunn, R., & Dunn, K. (1972). Learning styles/teaching styles: Should they ... can they ... be matched? *Educational Leadership, 36,* 2238-2244.

Friedman, C.P., & Stritter, F.T. (1976, November). An empirical inventory comparing instructional preferences of medical and other professional students. Research in Medical Education Proceedings 15th Annual Conference (pp. 63-68). San Francisco, CA.

Galbraith, M., & James, W. (1985). *Perceptual learning styles: Implications and techniques for the practitioner.* Washington, DC: American Association for Adult and Continuing Education.

Gardenswartz, L., & Rowe, A. (1993). *Managing diversity: A complete desk reference and planning guide.* New York: Irwin Pfeiffer & Company.

Gardner, R.W., Holzman, P.S., Klein, G.S., Linton, H. B., & Spence, D. (1959). *Cognitive control: A study of individual consistencies in cognitive behavior.* New York: International Universities Press.

Grasha, A.F., & Reichman, S.W. (1975). *Student Learning Styles Questionnaire.* Cinncinnati, OH: University of Cinncinnati Faculty Resource Center.

Guild, P. (1994). The culture/learning style connection. *Educational Leadership, 51-8,* 16-21.

Hodgkinson, H.L. (1985). Demographics and the economy: Understanding a changing marketplace [special issue on Adult Recruitment] *The Admissions Strategist: Recruiting for the 1980's.* New York: The College Board.

Hofstede, G. (1980). *Culture's consequences: International differences in work-related values.* Beverly Hills, CA: Sage.

Hudson Institute. (1988). *Opportunity 2000: Creative affirmative action strategies for a changing workforce.* Indianapolis, IN: The Institute.

Jonassen, D.H. (1994, April). Thinking technology: Toward a Constructivist design model, *Educational Technology,* pp. 34-37.

Jonassen, D.H. & Grabowski, B.L. (1993). *Handbook of individual differences learning and instruction.* Hillsdale, N.J.: Lawrence Erlbaum & Associates, Publishers.

Kagan, J. (1964). *Matching Familiar Figures Test.* Cambridge, MA: Harvard University.

Kagan, J. (1965). Impulsive and reflective children: Significance of conceptual tempo. In J. Krumboltz (Ed.), *Learning and the educational process,* (pp. 133-161), Chicago: Rand McNally.

Kagan, J. (1966). Developmental studies in reflection and cognitive performance. In A.H. Kidd & P. Mussen (Eds.), *Perceptual development in children,* (pp. 487-522). New York: International University Press.

Kirby, J. (1988). Style, strategy and skill in reading. In R.R. Schmeck (Ed.). *Learning strategies and learning styles,* (pp. 229-274). New York: Plenum.

Kolb, D.A. (1977). *Learning Styles Inventory: A self description of preferred learning mode.* Boston: McBer & Co.

Lowenfeld, V. (1946). *Creative and mental growth.* New York: Macmillan.

Moore, M.G. 1989. Editorial: Three types of interaction. *The American Journal of Distance Education,* 3(2): 1-6.

Myers, I.B. (1962). *The Myers-Briggs Type Indicator.* Palo Alto, CA: Consulting Psychologists Press.

Paivio, A. (1971). *Imagery and verbal processing.* New York: Holt, Rinehold & Winston.

Pask, G. (1988). Learning strategies, teaching strategies, and conceptual or learning style. In R. R. Schmeck (Ed.), *Learning strategies and learning styles,* (pp. 83-100). New York: Plenum Press.

Reichman, S.W., & Grasha, A. (1976). A rational approach to developing and assessing the construct validity of a student learning styles scales instrument. *The Journal of Psychology,* 87, 213-223.

Rezler, A.G. & Rezmovich, V. (1981). The learning preference inventory, *Journal of Allied Health,* 10, 28-34.

Richardson, A. (1977). Verbalizer-visualizer: A cognitive style dimension. *Journal of Mental Imagery,* 1, 109-126. Cited in Jonassen, D.H. & Grabowski, B.L. (1993), *Handbook of individual differences, learning and instruction.* Hillsdale, N.J: Lawrence Erlbaum & Associates, Publishers.

Rodriguez, F. (1988). Minorities and the school system, In R.A. Gorton, G.J. Schneider, & J.C. Fisher (Eds.), *Encyclopedia of school administration and supervision,* (pp. 172-173). Phoenix, AZ: Oryz Press.

Ross-Gordon, J. (1991). Needed: A multicultural perspective for adult education research. *Adult Education Quarterly,* 42-1, 1-16.

Sanchez, I.M. (1996). *An analysis of learning style constructs and the development of a profile of Hispanic adult learners.* Unpublished Doctoral dissertation. The University of New Mexico.

Sanders, J.A. & Wiserman, R.L. (1990). The effects of verbal and non-verbal teacher immediacy on perceived cognitive, affective and behavioral learning in the multicultural classroom. *Communication Education,* 39, 341-363.

Santostefano, S. (1964). Developmental study of the cognitive control "leveling-sharpening." *Merrill-Palmer Quarterly,* 10, 343-360.

Schmeck, R.R. (1988). Strategies and style of learning: an integration of varied perspective. In R.R. Schmeck (Ed.), *Learning strategies and learning styles,* (pp. 317-347). New York: Plenum Press.

Schmeck, R. R., Ribich, F., & Ramanaiah, N. (1977). Development of a self-report inventory for assessing individual differences in learning processes. *Allied Psychological Measurement,* 1, 413-431.

Smith, A. (1986, Ocotober). Stratefies for individualizing instruction across the disciplines for the culturally diverse learner. In *Thinking across the disciplines.* Proceedings of the Annual conference of the International Society for Individualized Instruction. Atlanta, GA.

Swassing, R. & Barbe, W. (1979). *The Swassing-Barbe Modality Index.* Columbus, OH: Zaner-Bloser.

Torrence, E.P., & Rockenstein, Z.L. (1988). Styles of thinking an creativity. In R.R. Schmeck (Ed.), *Learning strategies and learning styles,* (pp. 275-290). New York: Plenum Press.

Valdivieso, R. 7 Davis, C. (1988). *U.S. Hispanics: Challenging issues for the 1990's.* Washington, DC: Population Reference Bureau.

Weinstein, C.E. (1987). *LASSI users Manual.* Clearwater, FL: Holt Publish - ing Co.

Witkin, H.A. (1978). *Cognitive styles in personal and cultural adaptation.* Worchester, MA: Clark University Press.

Witkin, H.A., Moore, C.A., Goodenough, D.R., & Cox, P.W. (1977). Field dependent and field independent cognitive styles and their educational implications. *Review of Educational Research,* 47, 1-64.

Witkin, H.A., Oldman, P.K., Raskin, E., & Karp, S.A. (1971). *A manual for the Embedded Figures Tests.* Palo Alto, CA: Consulting Psychologists Press.

Chapter 4

The distance learner's academic self-concept

Chère Campbell Gibson

Persistence continues to be a concern among distance educators and administrators alike, indicated by the number of research studies related to this phenomenon (Cookson, 1990). The primary focus of these studies is the identification of influences on learners' decisions to leave distance education courses of study before completion (attrition).

In response to practitioner interest in persistence, a number of models have emerged to explain and predict attrition. These models include not only those characteristics students bring to the educational process at the time of entry, such as educational preparation, motivational and persistence attributes, and educational preparation (Kennedy and Powell, 1976; Sweet, 1986; Billings 1988), but also variables that are more situational in nature. These include the learner's life situation, such as family and employer support for studies and changes in life circumstances (Powell, Conway and Ross, 1990; Pythian and Clements, 1982: Woodley and McIntosh, 1980) and factors related to the educational institution, such as quality and difficulty of instructional materials and provision of tutorial support (Billings, 1988; Sweet, 1986; Kennedy and Powell, 1976).

One construct that emerges in a number of persistence studies pertains to an adult's perception of his or her ability to succeed in the educational environment. For example, Garrison (1985) studied whether goal clarity and course relevance variables would provide greater discrimination between persisters and nonpersisters in an adult basic education class than would other psychosocial variables. He concluded that, after the variables of last grade completed and hours worked entered the discriminant analysis, an ideal self/self-confidence discrepancy variable was the most powerful discriminator. Similarly, in a post hoc study of adults pursuing baccalaureate degrees at a distance, measures of expectancy of success in learning activities, as well as both dispositional (related to one's attitude and perceptions about self as learner) and independent study (related to the process of studying at a distance) variables were associated with persistence (Gibson and Graff, 1992). The Gibson and Graff (1992) findings closely parallel the Powell, Conway, and Ross (1990) findings with students' perception of their chances for success, value of previous education, concrete study habits, persistent behaviors, and need for support included in a discriminant model.

But what do we know about academic self-concept? How can we influence this important construct to enhance the potential for success in higher education at a distance? What can we do as educators to enhance a learner's academic self-concept? Perhaps some thoughts from adult learners pursuing baccalaureate degrees at a distance coupled with research findings of others can provide some useful insights.

Academic Self-Concept — A Dynamic and Multifaceted Construct

One key finding in the literature (Gibson and Graff, 1992; Graff and Coggins, 1989; Herrmann, 1988) relates to the dynamic nature of one's self-concept as a learner. For example, one student, reflecting on her levels of confidence entering her baccalaureate degree program and her level after completion of several course requirements, noted:

> Getting back and doing a few things and finding out ... that I'm not going to fail. I don't think it's going to be a problem getting through it as far as learning on my own. From that point of view ... I feel a lot more confident.

On a less positive note, and illustrating that some students may enter distance education programs with an inflated sense of their abilities and commitment to learn at a distance, another student stated:

Once I looked at the course material for geography and once I started this whole thing of realizing how much time I was willing to commit to it, I went from being fully confident [10] to where I am now [6]. (Reference to scale was this student's attempt to help the researcher understand the magnitude of her change in self-confidence.)

Not only did learners appear to reference time as they reflected on their perception of their abilities to successfully engage in a degree program at a distance, they also appeared to be thinking of several areas of competence. Some commented on their ability to cope with the process of learning as an adult. For example:

I thought that my weakness would be that at 41 maybe my retention power wouldn't be as great as it was ... in my last college days.

Others focused more specifically on their new roles as learners at a distance. One stated:

I quickly realized it was going to be a lot harder than I anticipated, so I went to an easier course ... so that I would gain some confidence in this whole way of learning.

Still others commented on their confidence relative to a body of content. For example, when asked directly about her level of confidence, one student said, "Once I get over the math class, pretty good!" On a more positive note, another student, as she reflected on her subject matter competence in a specific course, quipped, "I was surprised at how much I actually did know, did remember from years before!"

Thus we see a dynamic academic self-concept changing with time and experience. Facets of academic self-concept in higher education at a distance appear to include: the process of learning as an adult; the process of learning at a distance; and a content-specific aspect of academic self-concept. These facets may parallel what one would expect with the adult learner returning to our institutions to pursue a degree after some absence from school. The difference for our distance learner is that there is an additional issue — learning how to learn at a distance. They recognize this will be a new way of pursuing an education and are appropriately concerned that they may not be well-equipped to succeed in this new venue.

Enhancers and Detractors
of Academic Self-Concept

The literature and the voices of our learners at a distance help us recognize that there are both enhancers and detractors affecting the students' perception of self as learner at a distance. Many of these are environmental in origin and most are institutionally oriented.

Process-related factors affecting academic self-concept. A variety of confidence enhancers were mentioned as students reflected on the process of learning at a distance. Empathy on the part of the professors was noted as an enhancer.

> My confidence has been enhanced because the professors are so accommodating ... in this situation. The thing that is so wonderful is that they respect the position I'm in (as a working parent).

Personal success also appeared to play a large role in bolstering confidence and commitment as evidenced by such expressions as: "I feel like I'm absorbing all this stuff real well. I don't feel lost at all, you know, 'cause that would make me give up." Progress toward a larger educational goal also raised self-confidence. "If anything, I have been studying more now that I'm getting near the end of the course 'cause I feel so good that ... Hey, I think I've actually tackled one (course)."

Another student suggested, "The more you do the easier it gets." Another echoed the common refrain that familiarity with the process of learning at a distance enhances one's competence and confidence. Some noted that this familiarity with learning at distance comes as a result of trial and error, as exemplified by one student noting:

> I feel more competent in the sense that I'm getting to know what to expect 'cause when you first go in ... nobody really talks to you and says well maybe you should do this and this.

Self-growth also appeared to be an enhancer, as exemplified by this statement:

> Sitting down and having to feel that I am actively pursuing (knowledge) and kind of pushing out my boundaries and becoming. ... You can't but be a better person for it. And I actually enjoy that and ... that feeds your self-confidence, self-esteem.

What appears to emerge is a sense of accomplishment and a concomitant growing respect for one's self as learner.

On the flip side of the coin, students express a lack of confidence in themselves due to their lack of familiarity with the process and related roles in distance learning, with its separation of teacher and learner, increased learner responsibility, and autonomy. For example, one student noted, "Maybe after I finish a couple of courses, I'll be more confident and ... know what to do in certain situations."

Skill deficiencies also seemed related to levels of confidence. One student questioned her ability to learn and attributed this lack of confidence as follows. "Part of it is having really rusty study skills. Part of it is never having had study skills." Another noted, "I don't know if I can read well enough, although I have no trouble reading." Perhaps she reflected a need to identify some source for lack of confidence in her ability to succeed in the heavily print-based academic program in which she was enrolled.

Students' confidence in their ability to successfully complete a degree seemed directly related to their ability to juggle multiple roles, such as "trying to balance the stress of still getting my job done and coming home and studying" and "juggling time a little better." As one student reflected on her struggles to balance commitment to personal life with her commitment to learning, she confided:

> My biggest weakness is time. Wanting to maintain my personal life and my interests and activities and yet realizing that if I'm seriously going to get through this coursework ... I have to work at this every, at least every, day.

Thus, students expressed apprehensions about their ability to cope with a new process of learning. Included were concerns about their entering study skills and reading competencies, and ability to assume the new roles and responsibilities needed to succeed when learning at a distance. Again we see a close parallel to the concerns of the returning adult learner on campus but with the additional distance education process concerns.

Content-related factors affecting academic self-concept. Students also reflected on mastering a variety of content. They mentioned enhancers to academic self-concept (such as a new awareness of prior knowledge) after successfully taking a number of placement examinations — "I knew more than I thought I would know." Realization that their accumulated experience base was relevant also appeared to enhance confidence:

> After ... taking two exams that I took, I realize that I do know something. I'm not just picking it up right now. It's relating back to my present occupation and I'm very confident now ... everything isn't totally new. So the life experience that I had so far is helping.

After being probed about why she felt her confidence level was higher now than in the prior month, a student noted:

> The fact that I'm actually doing it as opposed to thinking about it (pursuing the degree). That I'm getting good feedback and some good grades and I'm accomplishing what I set out to do.

Success in mastering content enhances confidence. Related to that success is a familiarity with instructor expectations for testing and grading in a particular content area. For example, "Now that I've done a few assignments and taken a few tests in my two courses, I have a better idea of what they want and I feel more confident that I can do the work." Thus students' recognition of these content-related factors also appears to enhance their academic self-concept.

However, many students interviewed mentioned the same factors as detractors to their academic self-concept. Many of these detractors related to expectations regarding assignments, test taking, and test types. For example: "I think my biggest challenge was talking, having that initial conference with the instructors and finding out what they expected of me." One student noted, "I try to look at instructions and do what they say verbatim, but," she continued discouragedly, "sometimes you get off on a course (direction) that you think is appropriate but it really isn't." Some students even lacked sufficient confidence in their ability to guess what the instructor really wanted. They were reluctant to send in any assignments for fear they had guessed wrong. As one student explained: "So I know I need to send it (the completed assignment), just go ahead and do it, send it. Because if it isn't what they want they can let me know."

Also, students expressed diminished confidence in their academic abilities as they confronted a dreaded course. For example: "I'm pretty confident. I mean I'm still scared about the Logo one (computer course on LogoWriter)." An unfamiliar exam format, for example, also diminishes confidence. "I've never taken an oral exam before. I don't know what to expect." A student who was doing well and getting A's noted, "But, it's like I want to know why I got an A," expressing a need for feedback, insights into evaluation criteria, and perhaps data upon which to make an appropriate judgment about how confident she should be.

Registering for too many courses, then failing to make adequate progress also is a detractor. Reflecting on her waning commitment to learning and seeking a boost, a student commented, "I was going to call my adviser this week ... to ask what happens if, having bitten off 12 credits and wondering ... if I could finish it all in a year."

Progress toward degree completion was delayed by these detractors to academic self-concept, which led to further delay because the students were then hesitant to mail in completed assignments. Not meeting previously established academic goals also lowered the students' academic self-concept.

Strategic Intervention

Given the importance of students' academic self-concept to persistence and success in higher education at a distance, a better understanding of the nature of the construct and the influences of this facet on general self-concept becomes apparent. Academic self-concept of the distance learner appears to vary along a continuum from positive to negative and it also changes, with students becoming more or less confident/competent as they progress in their studies. Further, academic self-concept is multifaceted, related to both the process and the content of learning within the larger context of learning at a distance. Most important, academic self-concept appears to be a situational attribute of the learner, with specific institutional factors, emerging as influences.

How do we intervene? Can we institute procedures that can enhance the potential for success and minimize the barriers to successful completion? Ever the optimist, the answer is yes!

Analyses of the literature and the voices of distance learners in higher education provide ample support for continuing a number of already suggested, although not widely used, practices.

Process-related strategies to enhance academic self-concept. One strategy to address the process-related facet of academic self-concept is a student orientation. This orientation should provide an introduction to procedures for learning at a distance, including roles and responsibilities of teachers and learners. Instruction regarding the process of directing one's own learning and study strategies also seems appropriate early in a student's program.

Distance education, with the separation of teacher and learner — and often learner from peers — places considerable control for learning in the learner's hands. However, as Garrison and Baynton (1990) note, when given the opportunity to control their own learning, learners may not only be unwilling to assume the level of control required, but also lack the ability to assume the responsibilities associated with being a self-directed learner. The learner's past learning strategies are not always successful and a limited repertoire of learning strategies provides limited choices to deal with a new educational situation, such as learning at a distance.

Educational experiences that touch on adult development, especially learning in adulthood and learning how to learn, should be incorporated where possible. Optional time management and stress management programs also seem indicated, to help the student juggle his or her life as student with roles and responsibilities in work, family, and community.

The parallel to the on-campus adult learner is evident, but the workshops on strategic learning — including setting personal educational goals, learning new study skills and learning strategies, time and stress management, etc. — may be inaccessible for your distance learner. They may not be able to come to campus due to geographic distance and other barriers to participation, such as daytime scheduling of these workshops, the need for childcare, etc. How accessible are your current sources to enhance learning? Which could be delivered at a distance with a little creativity?

Content-related strategies to enhance academic self-concept. Of particular importance regarding learning specific content is the need for clearly outlined expectations on the part of the instructor. A variety of strategies can be put into place to overcome the anxiety and self-doubt that seems to emerge in our returning distance learner. These include signposts indicating important points for students' special attention to further assist learning. Sample questions and appropriate answers, given from the instructor's perspective, also help. Even samples of exemplary assignments or less-than-exemplary assignments with comments indicating areas for improvement seem indicated to help learners judge the quality of their work, if only against the teacher's criteria.

This call for clear instructor expectations of their students occurs during a period in distance education's history when there is a growing emphasis on providing increased learner control and less teacher-centered instruction (Evans and Nation, 1989). Multistage models are emerging with the goal of assisting students to become more self-directed in their learning over the course of their studies (Kasworm, 1992). Of particular concern is that, while a number of students expressed growing confidence in their ability to study successfully at a distance, these same students raised serious doubts about their competence and confidence relative to one or more bodies of content. This dichotomy appears consistent with the conceptualization of academic self-concept as increasingly less stable as one proceeds toward more specific aspects of subject matter and specific situations related to that subject matter (Shavelson, Hubner, and Stanton, 1976).

One strategy is to encourage learners to recognize the need to assess their own personal needs and tailor a course (within limits) to meet their learning goals and expectations. Faculty need to appreciate that many learners may lack the necessary level of confidence and perceived competence for this degree of self-directedness at initial stages of their program. However, given the situation specific nature of academic self-concept, it is important to provide options in which students could elect to take greater or lesser control over learning goals, methods, and evaluation strategies in all courses, whether the course level is introductory or advanced. As Bernard and Amundsen (1989) so aptly point out in their research, any institutional model of instructional design and learner support that advocates increasing student autonomy over time will fail to meet the need for direction and support for the student who lacks confidence and perceives a lack in competence for a specific subject or aspect of a subject toward the end of study.

One point was stressed repeatedly in the words of these students and those represented in earlier studies (e.g., Graff and Coggins, 1989): the difficulty of making that first phone contact with the professor to ask a question. Students continually voiced the need to be prepared, so as not to "sound like an idiot." It would seem that in higher education programs where learners are isolated from other learners, for example in print- and tape-based distance education programs, that an instructor-initiated phone contact during the first three weeks to ask if the student had any concerns indeed might answer a number of students' questions (related to such areas as expectations and educational processes), thereby enhancing academic self-concept and perhaps encouraging the submission of written assignments.

Further, feedback on assignments seems important, if only to help students assess their strengths and weaknesses and to judge more realistically their abilities. Self-assessment tools imbedded in study materials also bolster students' confidence by indicating when they are ready to take an exam based on their scores on similar self-testing devices. In addition, the nature of examinations needs to be specified. Hints also might be included, particularly for less familiar types of examinations such as the oral exam.

Conclusions

Academic self-concept is but one construct affecting the success of learners pursuing higher education degrees at a distance. However, as Snow (1989) notes in his discussion of cognitive and conative structures in learning, one needs to consider the initial states of learners, their desired end states, and the transitions between these states, given the impact of instruction to impact the transition from initial to end states. What becomes clear is that "achievements become aptitudes for further learning, and knowledge, skill, strategy, regulation and motivation intermingle; all have both cognitive and conative aspects" (p. 9).

The need to more fully develop and validate this construct is apparent, as well as is the need to develop measurement approaches to assess it. If a reliable and valid measure could be designed, one which takes into consideration the adult as learner, the educational program content, and the context of distance education, it could be used to identify learners who are potentially "at risk" of failure. The distance teaching organization then could target intervention and empowerment strategies to those most in need. Further, measuring the effectiveness of these individual intervention strategies would be facilitated by excluding those who neither need nor want additional or special services, either from the outset of their studies or at specific points during the course of their educational pursuits.

Research suggests that academic self-concept plays an important role in persistence in distance education and that this facet of general self-concept is a dynamic and situational attribute of the distance learner, and one that is amenable to intervention. Institutional practices can affect this all-important variable. With simple modifications in educational practices, the potential exists to enhance the learner's success in academic pursuits.

References

Bernard, R. M., & Amundsen, C. L. (1989). Antecedents to dropout in distance education: Does one model fit all? *Journal of Distance Education*, 4(2), 25-46.

Billings, D. M. (1988). A conceptual model of correspondence course completion. *The American Journal of Distance Education*, 2(2), 23-35.

Cookson, P. (1990). Persistence in distance education. In M.G. Moore (Ed.), *Contemporary issues in American distance education*, (pp. 192-203). Elmsford, New York: Pergamon Press, Inc.

Evans, T., & Nation, D. (Eds.) (1989). *Critical reflections on distance education*. London: Falmer Press.

Garrison, R., & Baynton, M. (1990). Beyond independence in distance education: The concept of control. *American Journal of Distance Education*, 1(3), 3-15.

Garrison, R. (1985). Predicting dropout in adult basic education settings: Interaction effects among school and nonschool variables. *Adult Education Quarterly*, 36(1), 25-38.

Gibson, C., & Graff, A. (1992). Impact of adults' preferred learning styles and perception of barriers on completion of external baccalaureate degree programs. *Journal of Distance Education*, 7(1), 39-51.

Graff, A., & Coggins, C. (1989). Twenty voices. In *Proceedings: Adult Education research conference* (pp. 159-164). Madison: University of Wis - consin-Madison.

Herrmann, A. (1988). A conceptual framework for understanding the transitions of perceptions of external degree students. *Distance Education*, 9(1), 5-26.

Kasworm, C. (1992). The development of adult learner autonomy and self-directedness in distance education. In *Proceedings: XVI World Conference of the International Council on Distance Education*. Bangkok, Thailand: Stou.

Kennedy, D., & Powell, R. (1976). Student progress and withdrawal in the Open University. *Teaching at a distance*, 7 (November), 61-75.

McIntosh, N. E., Woodley, A., & Morrison, V. (1980). Student demand and progress at the Open University: The first eight years. *Distance Education*, 1(1), 37-60.

Marsh, H. (1992). Content specificity of relations between academic achievement and academic self-concept. *Journal of Educational Psychology*, 84(1), 35-42.

Marsh, H., Byrne, B., & Shavelson, R. (1988). A multifaceted academic self-concept: Its hierarchical structure and its relation to academic achievement. *Journal of Educational Psychology*, 80(3), 366-380.

Powell, R., Conway, C., & Ross, L. (1990). Effects of student predisposing characteristics on student success. *Journal of Distance Education*, 5(1), 5-19.

Pythian, T., & Clements, M. (1982). Dropout from third level math courses. *Teaching at a Distance*, 21, 33-45.

Shavelson, R. J., Hubner, J.J., & Stanton, G.C. (1976). Self-concept: Validation of construct interpretations. *Review of Educational Research*, 46, 407-442.

Snow, R. E. (1989). Toward assessment of cognitive and conative structures in learning. *Educational Researcher*, 18(9), 8-14.

Sweet, R. (1986). Student dropout in distance education: An application of Tinto's model. *Distance Education*, 7(2), 201-213.

Woodley, A., & McIntosh, N. (1980). *The door stood open: An Evaluation of the open university young student pilot scheme*. London: Falmer Press.

Chapter 5

Improving learning outcomes: The effects of learning strategies and motivation

Christine H. Olgren

Introduction

To design effective distance education programs, it is important to understand how learning occurs and the factors that influence the learning process. Approaches to course design, however, often emphasize teaching strategies from an instructional perspective that assumes good teaching will produce good learning. The assumption that learning is a direct result of teaching overlooks years of research that has found many factors influence how the learner responds to instruction (Shuell, 1986).

If learning is the goal of education, then knowledge about how people learn should be a central ingredient in course design. As Morrison (1989) observed, removing barriers to effective learning and improving the quality of learning outcomes begins with the question, "What and how are people learning and what affects that process?"

This paper describes three factors that have a major impact on learning: (1) cognitive learning strategies for processing information, (2) metacognitive activities for planning and self-regulation, and (3) the learner's goals and motivations. The paper also discusses some implications for course designs and teaching methods in distance education.

Background: A Learning Strategy Perspective

Any approach to instructional design should be grounded in a theory or conception of the teaching-learning process. A theory, if explicitly stated and informed by research and practice, is a source of guidelines for design decisions. Without a guiding conception, instructional design is reduced to a set of techniques or procedures (Winn, 1990).

A guiding conception provides a framework that enables the designer to identify the major factors that influence learning and how those factors may interact with the design and teaching methods. However, a conception also includes beliefs about the nature of learning that may be tacit and unexamined. As Schon (1983) advised, the reflective practitioner should be aware of how core beliefs influence perspectives on learning and design.

The perspective put forth in this paper draws from learning strategy research in cognitive psychology, which focuses on how people mentally process information and construct knowledge in memory. The research relates learning strategies to the skills needed for knowing how to learn and to be self-directed.

Learning strategies are defined as thoughts and behaviors intended to influence how a person learns, thinks, and motivates himself or herself in order to carry out a learning task (Weinstein and Mayer, 1986). Studies indicate that capable learners use various cognitive strategies to select, organize, and integrate information as well as metacognitive strategies to plan and regulate learning. Ultimately, capable learners are said to be self-directed in having the capacity to design and carry out their own learning activities (Thomas and Rohwer, 1986; Derry and Murphy, 1986; Glaser, 1990).

Most learning strategy theory is based on a constructivist perspective, which contends that meaning and knowledge are constructed by the learner through a process of relating new information to prior knowledge and experience. Learning is viewed as an active, purposeful, and mean-ing-generating process that occurs within the learner (Shuell, 1986). In other words, learning involves the transformation of information into meaningful knowledge, where cognitive strategies serve to activate mental processes and prior knowledge to generate meaning from learning events (Jonassen, 1985).

Thus, the core beliefs underlying this paper are:

1. Research on the learning process helps us to understand how and what people learn. This understanding can be applied to course design to improve learning outcomes.

2. Learning involves an active search for meaning and understanding in relation to one's prior knowledge, experience, and interests. The more learners are actively involved in constructing relationships between new information and prior knowledge, the more likely they will be to learn and remember it.

3. Active learning requires interaction between learner and the material. Thus, to foster active learning, course designs should foster interaction.

4. Knowledge cannot be delivered to the learner. Knowledge is constructed by the learner through an active mental process of organizing, integrating, and applying new information.

5. The quality of learning outcomes depends on how well the learner organizes and integrates the information.

6. Mental engagement in learning is influenced by a variety of factors, including metacognition and motivation.

Cognitive Learning Strategies

Studies have found that learning involves four types of cognitive strategies that learners use to mentally process information (Olgren, 1992; Weinstein and Mayer, 1986; Pintrich, 1988):

1. Selection strategies, to focus attention and to identify relevant information

2. Rehearsal strategies, to remember information through repetition

3. Organization strategies, to build connections between new units of information

4. Elaboration strategies, to build connections between new information and what is already known

Table 1 lists common examples of these four cognitive strategies.

In selecting what to learn, students must be able to differentiate relevant from irrelevant material. To do this, learners use two kinds of selection strategies: (1) external focusing, on cues provided in a textbook or study guide or by the instructor to identify what the author, designer, or instructor thinks important to learn; or (2) internal focusing, on the learner's own needs and interests to identify information important to the learner. In formal education settings, learners focus primarily on external cues, such as bold print in a textbook or a list of course objectives, to identify material to learn for assessment. Far fewer students focus on their own needs or interests. Assessment demands, therefore, have a major influence on where attention and effort are focused.

Selection Strategies

Function: To focus attention and to identify relevant information

Examples: Focusing externally on text cues or study guide aids, focusing internally on personal needs and interests

Rehearsal Strategies

Function: To remember information by repetition

Examples: Memorizing, repeating, highlighting, copying, reading aloud, reviewing

Organization Strategies

Function: To build confidence an connections within the information given

Examples: Determining main ideas and relationships, outlining, listing, classifying, ordering, diagramming, comparing, contrasting, getting an overview, structured notetaking

Elaboration Strategies

Function: To expand the meaning and to build connections to prior knowledge/experience

Examples: Paraphrasing, summarizing, visualizing, associating ideas with examples, generative notetaking, creating analogies or metaphors, relating to prior learning, applying to work or everyday life, role-playing, brainstorming, reflecting, inferencing, evaluating usefulness, discussing, questioning, explaining, problem-solving

---

Table 1: Types of Cognitive Strategies

After information is selected and added to working memory, it must be processed for meaning. One function of rehearsal is to hold information in working memory, which has a rapid forgetting rate. However, rehearsal strategies may also be used as rote learning strategies for the verbatim reproduction of information. Because rehearsal strategies involve simply repeating and reproducing information, they result in little meaningful understanding or retention. As Marton and Saljo (1984) stated, students may work hard to memorize information, yet they fail to remember very much or for very long because the information means little to them.

Organization strategies are primarily directed at comprehending information by analyzing how ideas are structured and connected. That is, in order to comprehend the full meaning of new information, learners must be able to organize it logically — theme, main ideas, relationships among ideas, and supporting details or examples. As Kintsch (1989) observed, learners construct a mental model or representation of the information given, although it may vary in completeness. Because organization strategies focus on the information itself, they do not usually result in the active construction of external linkages for integration and application.

Elaboration strategies involve creating connections between new information and the learners' prior knowledge, experience, or interests. Elaboration strategies range from typical study strategies of paraphrasing and summarizing to higher-level strategies involving inferencing, analogical reasoning, reflective thinking, and applications to work or daily life. They entail expanding upon new information by relating it either directly or through analogy to what the learner already knows. Elaboration strategies, therefore, go beyond the information given to construct new meanings and to integrate information with prior knowledge in memory. In Kintsch's (1989) view, elaboration strategies reformulate or transform information by constructing a situated mental model linked into the learners' knowledge system. The elaboration process is considered critical for effective learning and deep understanding (Reigeluth and Stein, 1983; Mayer, 1984) and it enables learners to generalize and apply the material to other situations or to problem solving. However, because of their transformative nature, elaborations may not serve traditional assessment tasks that test for comprehension and retention.

The Quality of Learning

In addition to identifying mental activities, the concept of learning strategies draws attention to the quality of learning or how differences in the learning process affect the outcome. Quality is conceptualized as the level of understanding, integration, and application attained by the student.

Studies have found that rehearsal strategies involve shallow processing at a surface level of verbatim learning, while organization and elaboration strategies involve processing at deeper levels of understanding, integration, and application (Weinstein and Mayer, 1986; Dansereau, 1985; Pintrich and Johnson, 1990).

For deep learning to occur, then, students should use a combination of several organization and elaboration strategies to analyze (take apart) and synthesize (put together) information in ways that build a mental model linked to prior knowledge in memory. As Marton and Saljo (1976) found, learners who really understand material engage in destructuring the material, then restructuring it to relate the material to their existing knowledge system. In destructuring and restructuring the material, the learner engages in an active and reflective dialog with the material. Reflection, or pausing to think about the material, is a higher-level elaboration strategy that uses prior knowledge to make inferences and draw conclusions, a strategy characteristic of capable learners and problem-solvers (Alexander and Judy, 1988; Derry and Murphy, 1986).

Metacognitive Influences

To effectively use cognitive strategies, learners must know what the strategies are, when to use them, and how to apply them appropriately. Such knowledge is one aspect of metacognition.

Metacognition refers to the learners' awareness and knowledge of their own learning processes as well as their abilities and tendencies to control those processes (Derry and Murphy, 1986). Metacognition might be thought of as an "inner coach" who guides the learner in making decisions about how and what to learn.

Metacognition involves three key components:

- Awareness: awareness of how learning is being carried out
- Knowledge: knowledge about self, the learning task, and how one learns under different conditions
- Control: the ability and desire to plan and regulate the learning process

Learning with awareness, knowledge, and control sounds like an abstract process. However, it is readily observable by watching what learners do to control their learning. Metacognitive control activities involve a variety of behaviors for planning and managing the learning process (Table 2).

Preparing to Learn: Many metacognitive activities involve preparations for learning, or "orienting strategies." Orienting strategies include identifying required tasks, appraising the value or usefulness of the task, estimating the mental effort involved, establishing goals or a purpose for learning, and making a study plan. Preparing to learn, therefore, is a crucial first stage in which the learner's initial perceptions of the task and its value influence motivation, goal-setting, and decisions about the amount of time and mental effort to invest.

Students preparing to learn in formal education settings most often use the instructor's syllabus or study guide for information about course objectives, expectations, and requirements. Students may also skim content outlines, overviews, or main headings in reading materials. While such orientation aids are essential for clarification, they are also instrumental in activating extrinsic motivations for learning, particularly a concern for what is required to "make the grade." Students also use such

---

Functions:
   To plan, monitor, regulate, and evaluate learning

Orienting strategies (preparing to learn):
   Identifying required tasks and assessment demands
   Appraising relevance or usefulness
   Estimating time and mental effort
   Identifying goals
   Making a study plan
   Finding a comfortable place to study
   Locating resources
   Activating prior knowledge

Regulating strategies (monitoring the learning process):
   Checking comprehension
   Managing time and pacing
   Ajusting cognitive strategies to learning tasks
   Persisting in task engagement
   Checking for exam readiness by self-testing
   Seeking help
   Evaluating what was learned

Table 2: Types of Metacognitive Strategies

orientation aids to appraise the potential value of the learning task. If a learning task is perceived as irrelevant, boring, too difficult, or too trivial, a learner may find little intrinsic motivation for learning and may decide it is not worth the mental effort to engage in deep-level learning (Volet, 1991; Olgren; 1992; Marland et al, 1984).

Monitoring the Learning Process: Other metacognitive activities occur during the learning process. These activities most often involve monitoring progress and making adjustments in goals or mental effort. A term commonly used is "self-regulation strategies" (Zimmerman, 1990). Examples are checking comprehension, monitoring time and pacing, adapting cognitive strategies to learning demands, revising goals, persisting to task completion, seeking help, and self-testing to evaluate what was learned.

Individuals differ in metacognitive awareness, knowledge, and desire to control their learning. Awareness requires that the learner step back and consider his or her own learning process as an object of thought and reflection by consciously preparing to learn and by actively monitoring progress. Because attention is typically focused on the content rather than the process, learning often occurs rather automatically unless the individual encounters a problem or pauses to focus attention on the learning process itself.

In addition, many learners do not know enough about how to use cognitive strategies. The most effective learners have a larger repertoire of learning strategies. They are also aware of the need to employ strategies that fit the learning task and to change strategies if goals are not being achieved (Thomas and Rohwer, 1986; Pressley, Borkowski, and Schneider, 1987). Learners with the least strategy knowledge are the most apt to use rehearsal as a rote learning strategy to memorize information verbatim. They are also the least aware of the learning process, tending to employ rehearsal strategies in a largely habitual and unconscious way and to blame problems on something other than their learning strategies. In this sense, metacognitive capabilities involve accepting responsibility for learning or what Shuell (1988) describes as having an internal locus of responsibility.

Goals and Motivational Influences

Cognitive strategies cannot be divorced from the learnerr's purpose in using them. A strategy involves an action — a thought or behavior — directed toward accomplishing a goal or purpose. Cognitive strategies, then, are highly influenced by the learner's goals and motivations for learning. It is important to distinguish between cognitive goals and affective goals.

Cognitive goals relate to the level of learning or how deeply the student processes information. Rehearsal strategies are typically directed to goals of remembering information at a shallow level of verbatim processing. Organization and elaboration strategies are typically directed to goals of understanding and applying the material. They involve deeper processing at levels of application, analysis, synthesis, and evaluation.

Affective goals relate to intrinsic and extrinsic reasons for participating in a learning activity. Learners often have multiple aims, interests, and motives for learning that relate not only to the immediate learning task but also to broader concerns. A study by Taylor, Morgan, and Gibbs (1981) at the British Open University found that students had goals related to academic, vocational, and personal concerns (see Table 3). The goals could further be described as intrinsic or extrinsic. Intrinsic goals expressed a desire to learn the material for skill development, intellectual interests, challenge, or personal growth. Extrinsic goals were concerned with learning as a means to some other end, such as getting a good grade, completing academic requirements, and earning a degree for job promotion.

Research has shown that intrinsic goals are associated with deep approaches to learning that emphasize organization and elaboration strategies for understanding and applying the material. Extrinsic goals are associated with surface approaches to learning that emphasize rehearsal strategies to reproduce and remember discrete facts (Entwistle and Ramsden, 1983; Olgren, 1992). Thus, intrinsic motivation is critical to deep learning, presumably because learners are more willing to put forth the mental effort to really learn the material.

Implications for Course Design

Cognitive research on how and what students learn has important implications for the design of distance education programs. The quality of learning outcomes depends on how deeply the learner engages with new information to construct a meaningful knowledge structure — or mental model — that is integrated into memory. Such a knowledge structure involves more than simply comprehending new information. It also requires the active use of organizing and elaborating strategies to analyze and transform information into usable knowledge that can be applied to problem-solving or other situations.

How can course designs incorporate important research findings? Here are some implications and suggestions.

Approaches to Course Design: Most instructional design approaches are rooted in behavioral learning theory that advocates breaking down content or skills to be learned into measurable or observable subcomponents. Reducing outcomes to behavioral subcomponents is an analysis design strategy. The concentration on behavioral subcomponents also

Orientation	Interest	Aim	Concerns
Voctional	Intrinsic	Skill development	Relevance of course to career of job
	Extrinsic	Certification	Degree for job promotion or career advancement
Academic	Intrinsic	Intellectual achievement	Self-satisfaction, mastery, challenge
	Extrinsic	Educational advancement	Grades, academic requirements
Personal	Intrinsic	Self-improvement	Personal growth and enjoyment of learning
	Extrinsic	Proof of capability	Self-esteem or status
Social		Communication, association	Interpersonal relationships

Table 3: Intrinsic and Extrinsic Goal Orientations

tends to focus learning on cognitive goals of comprehension or skill acquisition. Winn (1990) warns that problems may occur when behavioral design strategies are used to teach content and skills that require higher levels of cognitive processing. As researchers have found, learning for higher cognitive goals require the student to both analyze (break down) and synthesize (put back together) information. Yet, design strategies that focus primarily on analysis overlook the need for synthesis.

A concentration on behavioral subcomponents or the acquisition of skill behaviors may also overlook the importance of students' knowledge structures. A crucial aspect of learning in cognitive theory is the development of mental models (Gentner and Stevens, 1983) that connect conceptual knowledge with procedural skills to enable both understanding and application.

If course designs are to incorporate both analysis and synthesis strategies to facilitate higher-level learning and the development of richly connected mental models, then course designers will need to know more about their learners' cognitive strategies and prior knowledge in the content area.

Needs Analysis: Most approaches to needs analysis in instructional design focus on content analysis or task analysis to identify what students should learn. If learners are assessed, the information gathered is usually about demographic characteristics and academic achievement. Because higher-level goals of understanding and application require learning processes that relate new information to prior knowledge, the designer should the entering students' knowledge about both content and process.

Information about content knowledge can be gathered through pre-assessments of students' knowledge and skills. Pretesting, however, is not always possible in distance education programs, and pretests may not reveal knowledge or experiences that can be applied to learning through analogical reasoning. Another solution is to create flexible course designs that use modular units, optional exercises, or modifiable teaching strategies to accommodate the differing knowledge levels of students. The use of collaborative activities, such as peer teaching or work-teams, also accommodates differing knowledge levels by having more-knowledgeable and less-knowledgeable students work together.

Information gathered about students' knowledge of the learning process should include their cognitive strategies, metacognitive strategies, and thinking skills. Such information is particularly important in distance education, where students often have more responsibility. Methods for assessing strategy knowledge and skills include the Motivated Strategies for Learning Questionnaire (Pintrich and DeGroot, 1990) and the Self-Regulated Learning Interview Schedule (Zimmerman and Martinez-Pons, 1986). Autobiographical storytelling, reflective journals, and thinking skills inventories are also useful tools.

Instructional Objectives and Activities: Instructional objectives traditionally focus on what is to be learned in the subject matter domain. Also important are objectives related to the learning process. Because outcomes depend largely on the learners' mental activities and motivations, instructional designs should include goals to: (1) foster mental involvement in learning, (2) foster emotional involvement in learning, and (3) develop learning skills in using cognitive and metacognitive strategies.

1. *To foster mental involvement in learning:* Course designs should include a variety of interactive or collaborative activities essential for active learning. Such activities can draw upon three types of interactions: (a) instructor-student, (b) student-student, and (c) student-material. The activity may be instructor-based, where it is embedded into the course design or guided by the instructor, or, learner-based, where the learners are asked to carry it out on their own.

Instructor-based activities include many guided learning methods for involving students in interaction or collaboration. These methods include discussion, problem-solving, brainstorming, case studies, simulations, debates, role plays, reactor panels, collaborative projects, and teamwork. Organization and elaboration strategies can also be designed into print materials by using orientation aids and elaboration aids (Mayer, 1984) or exercises and activities (Race, 1989; Rowntree, 1986). Learner-based activities ask the learners to engage in using organizing or elaborating strategies on their own in assignments, exercises, or outcome assessments. However, learner-based activities assume that learners know the strategies and can apply them effectively.

The purpose of interactive activities is to involve students in the kinds of analysis and synthesis processes essential for deep understanding and application. That is, the activities should engage students in using organization and elaboration strategies to take apart and put together information. In this sense, interactive course designs seek to emulate the active and reflective self-dialogues used by capable, deep-level learners. Such dialogues typically involve a self-questioning process similar to Socratic teaching methods or what Holmberg (1986) called carrying on a "reflective conversation" with the text.

Course design, therefore, involves much more than simply delivering content. Unfortunately, distance education programs often use technology as a distribution system to efficiently serve more students. While wider program distribution can provide new learning opportunities to students, it can result in course designs that emphasize content delivery methods rather than interactive learning activities. Dillon, Gunawardena, and Parker (1992), for example, found that 80% of the instructors in interactive video classrooms used primarily lecture methods.

2. *To foster emotional involvement in learning:* Course designs should include orientation aids or activities that help learners to identify the value of the material and their own intrinsic purposes for learning. Because the preparation stage of learning is crucial to learners' appraisals of motivational interests and goals, orientation aids or activities directed to the learner are important design features. Such aids should help learners to preview the material in relation to their needs, interests, and experiences. The aids should also ask learners to determine their own intrinsic goals as additions to the instructional objectives. Designers should not assume that their instructional objectives will be of intrinsic interest to the learner, and instructional objectives may invite extrinsic motivation and less mental effort if students perceive little value in the learning task. Intrinsic motivation can be supported by incorporating activities or elaboration strategies that involve students in actively creating links to their needs, interests, and knowledge. Motivation is also sustained by social learning processes of communication, collaboration, and a supportive atmosphere (Volet, 1991).

3. *To develop students' learning capacities:* For deep-level learning, students must use effective cognitive and metacognitive strategies. Not all students, however, have this capability. Learning deficiencies are particularly serious in distance education, which often requires that students take on more responsibility for their own learning. For example, independent study programs or learning via the World Wide Web often assume students have the knowledge, skills, and

desire to control their learning. However, problems of student persistence and completion suggest many learners are not prepared for self-paced programs.

Distance education programs commonly respond to learning deficiencies by offering traditional study skills advice or training directed to grades and assessment (e.g., Sammons and Kozoll, 1986; Northedge, 1990). However, study skills training that does not consider motivation or cognitive goals may result in little skill improvement (Morgan, Taylor, and Gibbs, 1982), low transfer to other contexts (Dansereau 1985), or an increase in surface learning if study skills are aimed at traditional assessment demands (Ramsden, Beswich, and Bowden, 1987).

More success has been reported with developing learners' cognitive and metacognitive strategies by support devices embedded in instruction (Valcke et al., 1993) and by cognitive apprenticeship models (Brown, Collins, and Duguid, 1989). For example, Volet (1991) describes the effectiveness of using a cognitive apprenticeship approach for modeling and coaching students in the metacognitive and cognitive strategies needed for self-regulated learning in a computer course. Embedded and modeling approaches can help students to learn a strategy through practice, but instruction should include complete explanations of the strategy, how, when, and where to use it, and the benefits.

4. *Assessment Methods:* If the desired outcome of learning involves higher-level goals of understanding and application, then assessment methods should enable students to demonstrate their developing knowledge structures and application skills. Such demonstration is difficult, if not impossible, in objective testing methods. Objective testing methods, such as multiple-choice examinations, most often focus on specific pieces or sub-components of course content, in keeping with analysis design strategies and comprehension goals. Objective testing does not enable students to express holistically the extent to which they have built a mental structure of interrelated concepts and procedural skills that is integrated in memory. Cognitive theorists, therefore, recommend other forms of authentic assessment that include case studies, projects, portfolios, investigations, interviews, and post-mortems of problem-solving episodes (McLellan,

1993). These methods enable students to not only express and apply their knowledge, but also to engage in active and reflective learning processes.

The notion of authentic assessment grows out of the belief that testing isolated components of knowledge does not effectively measure higher-level learning outcomes (Guba and Lincoln, 1989). Thus, authentic assessment methods are recommended in order to enable students to construct responses rather than select among pre-existing choices, to use higher-order thinking processes of analysis, synthesis, and application, and to demonstrate wholistic models or projects. Authentic assessment methods also encourage self-assessment to teach students how to evaluate and take control of their work. Assessment in general, therefore, is concerned with both the content and process of learning.

Summary

The research on learning strategies and motivations can benefit course design in distance education in several important ways. First, the research draws attention to the quality of learning outcomes and provides insights into how learning occurs. Second, the research suggests reasons why individual learners may not respond to instructional events as intended by the designer. Third, the research implies that course designs should aim to develop both content and process skills, while also attending to motivational influences. Finally, the research supports course designs that use a variety of interactive activities that engage the learner in analyzing, integrating, and applying information within a context of "real world" problems, case studies, or simulations. As Garrison (1993) stated, "Those of us that have the technology must design the learning process not just to learn information faster or easier but that will encourage and challenge learners to construct their own meaning and create new knowledge" (p. 207).

References

Alexander, P.A., & Judy, J.E. (1988). The interaction of domain-specific and strategic knowledge in academic performance. *Review of Educational Research* , 58(4), 375-404.

Brown, J.S., Collins, A., & Duguid, P. (1989). Situated cognition and the culture of learning. *Educational Researcher*, 18(1), 32-42.

Dansereau, D.F. (1985). Learning strategy research. In J.W. Segal & S.F. Chipman (Eds.) *Thinking and learning skills*, Vol. I, Hillsdale, NJ: Lawrence Erlbaum.

Derry, S.J., & Murphy, D.A. 986. Designing systems that train learning ability. *Review of Educational Research*, 56(1), 1-39.

Dillon, C.L., Gunawardena, C.N., & Parker, R. (1992). Learner support in distance education: An evaluation of a state-wide telecommunications system. *International Journal of Instructional Media*, 19 (4), 297-312.

Entwistle, N.J., & Ramsden, P. (1983). *Understanding student learning*. London: Croom Helm.

Garrison, D.R. (1993). A cognitive constructivist view of distance education: An analysis of teaching-learning assumptions. *Distance Education*, 14(2), 199-211.

Gentner, D., & Stevens, A. (Eds.). (1983). *Mental models* . Hillsdale, NJ: Lawrence Erlbaum.

Glaser, R. (1990). The reemergence of learning theory within instructional research. *American Psychologist*, 45(1), 29-39.

Guba, E.G., & Lincoln, Y.S. (1989). *Fourth generation evaluation*. Newbury Park, CA: Sage Publicatoins.

Holmberg, B. (1986). *Growth and structure in distance education*. London: Croom Helm.

Jonassen, D.H. 1985. Learning strategies: A new educational technology. *Programmed Learning and Educational Technology*, 22(1), 26-34.

Kintsch, W. (1989). Learning from text. In L.B. Resnick (Ed.), *Knowing, learning, and instruction: Essays in honor of Robert Glaser*. Hillsdale, NJ: Lawrence Erlbaum.

Marland, P., Patching, W., Putt, I., & Store, R. (1984). Learning from distance-teaching materials: A study of students' mediating responses. *Distance Education*, 5(2), 215-236.

Marton, F., & Saljo, R. (1984). Approaches to learning. In F. Marton, D. Hounsell, & N. Entwistle (Eds.), *The experience of learning*. Edinburgh: Scottish Academic Press.

Marton, F., & Saljo, R. (1976). On qualitative differences in learning: I. Outcomes and processes. *British Journal of Educational Psychology*, 46, 4-11.

Mayer, R.E. (1984). Aids to text comprehension. *Educational Psychologist*, 19(1), 30-42.

McLellan, H. (1993). Evaluation in a situated learning environment. *Educational Technology*, 33(3), 39-45.

Morgan, A.R., Taylor, E., & Gibbs, E. (1982). Variations in students' approaches to studying. *British Journal of Educational Technology*, 13(2), 107-113.

Morrison, T.R. (1989). Beyond legitimacy: Facing the future in distance education. *International Journal of Lifelong Education*, 8(1), 3-24.

Northedge, A. (1990). *The good study guide. Milton Keynes: Open University Educational Enterprises.*

Olgren, C.H. (1992). *Adults' learning strategies and outcomes in an independent study course.* Unpublished doctoral dissertation, University of Wisconsin-Madison, Madison, Wisconsin.

Pintrich, P.R. (1988). A process-oriented view of student motivation and cognition. In J.S. Sork & L.A. Mets (Eds.), *Improving teaching and learning through research.* New Directions for Institutional Research. No. 57. San Francisco: Jossey-Bass.

Pintrich, P.R., & DeGroot, E. (1990). Motivational and self-regulated learning components of classroom academic performance. *Journal of Educational Psychology*, 82(1), 33-40

Pintrich, P.R., & Johnson, G.R. (1990). Assessing and improving students' learning strategies. In *The Changing Face of College Teaching.* ed., M.D. Svinicki. New Directions for Teaching and Learning, 42, 83-92.

Pressley, M., Borkowski, J.G., & Schneider, W. (1987). Cognitive strategies: Good strategy users coordinate megacognition and knowledge. *Annals of Child Development*, 4, 89-129.

Ramsden, P., Beswick, D., & Bowden, J. (1987). Learning processes and learning skills. In J. Richardson, M. Eysenck, & D. Piper (Eds.), *Student Learning: Research in Education and Cognitive Psychology.* Milton Keynes: Open University Press.

Reigeluth, C., & Stein, F. (1983). The elaboration theory of instruction. In C.M. Reigeluth (Ed.). *Instructional-Design Theories and Models: An Overview of Their Current Status.* Hillsdale, NJ: Lawrence Erlbaum.

Race, P. (1989). *The open learning handbook: Selecting, designing, and supporting open learning materials*. New York: Nichols Publishing.

Rowntree, D. (1986). *Teaching through self-instruction: A practical hand - book for course developers*. London: Kogan Page.

Sammons, M., & Kozoll, C.E. (1986). *Making the grade: A how-to guide for completing self-study courses*. The Guide Series in Continuing Education, Urbana-Champaign: University of Illinois.

Schon, D.A. (1983). *The reflective practitioner* . New York: Basic Books.

Shuell, T.J. 1986. Cognitive conceptions of learning. *Review of Educational Research*, 56(4), 411-436.

Shuell, T.J. (1988). The role of the student in learning from instruction. *Contemporary Educational Psychology*, 13, 276-295.

Taylor, E., Morgan, A., & Gibbs, E. (1981). The orientation of Open University foundation students to their studies. *Teaching at a Distance*, 20, 3-12.

Thomas, J.W., & Rohwer, W.D., Jr. (1986). Academic studying: The role of learning strategies. *Educational Psychologist* , 21(1&2), 19-41.

Valcke, M.M.A., R.L. Martens, P.H.A.G. Poelmans, & M.M. Daal. (1993). The actual use of embedded support devices in self-study materials by students in a distance education setting. *Distance Education*, 14(1), 55-84.

Volet, S.E. (1991). Modeling and coaching of relevant metacognitive strategies for enhancing university students' learning. *Learning and Instruction*, 1, 319-336.

Weinstein, C.E., & Meyer, R.E. (1986). The teaching of learning strategies. In *Handbook of Research on Teaching*, 3rd edition, ed. M.C. Wittrock. New York: Macmillan.

Winn, W. (1990). Some implications of cognitive theory for instructional design. *Instructional Science*, 19, 53-69.

Zimmerman, B.J. (1990). Self-regulated learning and academic achievement: An Overview. *Educational Psychologist*, 25, 3-17.

Zimmerman, B.J. & Martinez-Pons, M. (1986). Development of a structured interview for assessing student use of self-regulated learning strategies. *American Educational Research Journal*, 23(4), 614-628.

Chapter 6

Learning in a networked world: New roles and responsibilities

Terry D. Anderson and D. Randy Garrison

Developments in communications technology are having a profound effect on both distance education and higher education in general. Technologies such as computer-mediated communication and learning networks are making collaborative and personalized learning experiences, at a distance, a reality. These same technologies and the growing pressure to provide quality learning experiences on-campus are also transforming higher education, particularly with regard to the dominance of the lecture.

Oblinger and Maruyama (1996) report that in higher education a "majority of institutions construe teaching almost entirely in terms of lecturing" (p. 2). Interestingly, this practice of focusing on the transmission of information shares similar characteristics to traditional distance education. Although the medium of transmission is different, both teaching and learning models are largely based upon one-way transmission of information with little chance for sustained interaction. In distance education the dominant model has attempted to maximize access through the mass production of self-instructional course materials (Garrison, 1997; 1995). In campus-based higher education, the lecture is also used to transmit information as efficiently as possible. However, developments in communications technologies are causing those in higher education to rethink teaching and learning. Communications technology that supports sustained interaction is having a significant impact in higher education — both on-campus and at a distance.

This chapter will explore the new roles and responsibilities for higher education teachers and learners in a communications technology environment. The discussion will first focus on the broad issues of communication, control, and collaboration. Then the full range of educational interactions will be identified and described in the context of learning networks.

Communication, Control, and Collaboration

To understand the new roles and responsibilities of teachers and learners, we must begin with a discussion of the nature of educational communication where personal meaning and continuous learning (learning how to learn) are intended outcomes. While it may seem obvious "that education depends upon acts of communication" (Salomon, 1981), not all communication fully qualifies as being educational. Educational communication in its best sense should be reciprocal (i.e., two-way), consensual (i.e., voluntary), and collaborative (i.e., shared control). Too often educational transactions are dominated by the one-way transmission of information without considering the process of constructing meaningful and worthwhile knowledge. Educational communication must facilitate the construction and negotiation of meaning, which is dependent upon critical discourse and knowledge confirmation. Educational communication must be explanatory and not just confirmatory. That is, it explains why a conception makes sense or not, as opposed to simply stating that it is right or wrong.

Communication for educational purposes should have an interactive component. This inherently shifts the balance of control. This balance of control is being shifted in higher education, as learners and society in general demand that learning be meaningful and relevant to changing needs, and in distance education, as a result of learning networks. The access and independence (where and when) characteristic of the industrial model of distance education provided little control and support with regard to what was to be learned and how it was to be assimilated. This excessive focus of distance education on independence as an ideal was questioned and the concept of control proposed (Garrison, 1989; 1995; Garrison and Baynton, 1987).

The control model attempted to reflect the complexity of the educational transaction. The control dynamics were placed in the context of a dynamic interaction among teacher, learner, and content, facilitated by unconstrained two-way communication. More specifically, control was seen as a subset of these macro-level components and consisted of three dimensions — independence, support, and proficiency (see Figure 1). In essence, "control" means having choices and making decisions as well as having the necessary contextual support and capability to successfully achieve the intended learning outcome. "Independence" reflects the freedom to choose and pursue desired learning goals. While independence may well be desirable, it may also be a mirage that results in more insidious forms of dependence. Independence may result in isolation and not produce worthwhile and expected learning outcomes. "Support" balances independence and reflects the range of human and non-human resources that can facilitate meaningful and worthwhile learning. "Proficiency" reflects the ability to construct meaning and the disposition needed to initiate and persist in a learning endeavor. The integrating process is the quality of the communication and collaboration

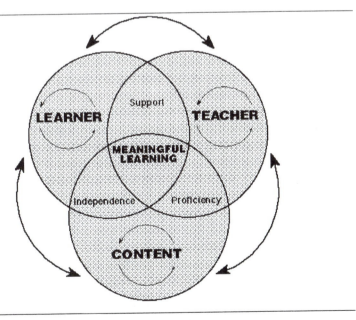

Figure 1: Transactional Relationships in Higher Education
(Adopted from Garrison, 1989)

as well as the balance of control among facilitator, learners, and curriculum.

The quality of the learning outcome is found at the center (intersection) of the overlapping macro- (teacher, learner, and content) and micro- (independence, support, and proficiency) level educational relationships reflected in Figure 1. If the three control dimensions are in dynamic balance, the resulting learning outcome will be personally meaningful as well as socially worthwhile. That is, the very purpose of attending to and balancing independence, support, and proficiency dimensions (i.e., control) is to facilitate meaningful and worthwhile learning outcomes. More specifically, by "meaningful" we mean that learners have assumed responsibility to make sense of the content through assimilating or accommodating new ideas and concepts into their existing knowledge structure. Worthwhile knowledge is that knowledge which has been consensually confirmed and which has redeeming social values.

In the educational context, meaningful and worthwhile learning goes beyond simply accessing information and control. Increasingly the issue is the quality of the learning experience — the ability to critically judge information and construct knowledge and action. The independence and isolation characteristic of the industrial era of distance education is being challenged by the collaborative approaches to learning made possible by learning networks. Moreover, educational theory is shifting to a collaborative constructivist conception of learning. This orientation recognizes that shared control is the prerequisite for a learner to assume responsibility to construct meaning. Responsibility "suggests an obligation for purposeful unconstrained participation of the individual in creating meaning ... through the critical analysis and integration of new ideas/values" (Garrison, 1993, p. 36). Responsibility is a key issue in a collaborative constructivist perspective of teaching and learning.

The constructivist perspective rejects the view that knowledge can be transmitted in whole from the teacher to the learner. Constructivist learning scenarios are complex and collaborative. They focus on individual responsibility to construct meaning as well as authentic reciprocal communication for the purposes of confirming understanding and generating worthwhile knowledge. Until recent times, collaborative constructivist approaches to learning at a distance were limited by the technology (audio/video teleconferencing), cost, and convenience. However, with the developments in integrating telecommunications and computer technologies, the resulting learning networks make it possible to offer collaborative learning experiences at a distance in a cost-effective manner. Sustained networked communication has become affordable to institutions of higher education and make it possible to offer a broad range of programs to learners without geographical boundary.

Types of Interaction

The previous model of transactional relationships (see Figure 1) suggests six possible types of interaction. At the intersection of the three macro-components exist the first set of interactions: learner-teacher, learner-content, and teacher-content. Within each of the macro-components exists another set of interactions: learner-learner, teacher-teacher, and content-content. It is interesting to note that Moore (1989) had previously identified three of the six interactions that emerged from the transactional relationships: learner-teacher, learner-content, and learner-learner. However, we believe that all types of interactions have importance in understanding the teaching-learning transaction. In the context of communications technologies, particularly learning networks, we discuss each of the six interactions. The issues of support, independence, and proficiency (i.e., control issues) guide the discussion within each type of interaction.

Learner-teacher interaction

Learner-teacher communication goes to the heart of education — both face-to-face and at a distance. Moore and Kearsley (1996) include interaction in their definition of distance education, which begins, "The transaction which we call distance education is the interplay between people who are teachers and learners" (p. 200). The physical distance separating learners and teachers in distance education contexts necessitates that this communication be mediated. Nearly every communication medium has been adapted, with varying degrees of success, to support this learner-teacher interaction. This challenge has led to the development of techniques and approaches designed to facilitate the learning interaction by minimizing any deleterious effects of the media and maximizing the potential for productive learning interactions. For example, Hardy and Olcott (1995) suggest learning activities such as advanced questions, paced group learning, and immediate reinforcement of learner input are particularly appropriate to audio teleconferenced interactions. Collins and Berge (1998) maintain a "Moderator's Home Page" (http://cac.psu.edu/~mauri/moderators.html) which contains links to resources aimed at helping both teachers and learners adapt to learning in computer-conferenced environments.

A key element in this dyad is support. Interaction between learner and teacher is essential to assess current understanding, design appropriate approaches (e.g., depth, pacing), stimulate critical reflection, and diagnose misconceptions. These elements of support are required whether educational communication is mediated technologically or occurs in a conventional face-to-face environment. While support elements are often neglected in campus-based higher education, they are usually absent in traditional distance education approaches. Support in campus- or distance-based higher education is dependent upon sustained two-way communication. Communications technology can support learning in campus-based or distance education.

Supporting learner-teacher interactions through technology requires access and opportunities to become proficient with the appropriate technology in use. The problems of providing access to, and support for, telecommunications has led many institutions and teachers to provide "optional" or "enrichment activities" for those learners who wish to use the technology. This approach, though laudable in its attempt to provide options for learners, is rarely successful, as learners sense the undervalued nature of the optional activity. In response, they often do not take the time and energy to create the necessary community of inquiry (Anderson, 1994). Opportunities to improve proficiencies in learning are lost.

Learner-learner interaction

Distance educators have traditionally defined interaction and support in terms of tutor, teacher, or institutional assistance provided to the individual learner. When one considers distance education contexts enriched by telecommunications tools used to support multiple forms of learner-learner and learner-teacher interactions, the concept of support, proficiency, and independence must be expanded to include learners supporting each other.

There is a growing literature base supporting the use of peer interaction in formal face-to-face educational settings. Damon (1984) noted that "intellectual accomplishments flourish best under conditions of highly motivated discovery, the free exchange of ideas and the reciprocal feedback between mutually respected individuals" (p. 340). Lipman (1991) emphasized the crucial importance of community in education and intellectual development. We argue that this learning community realized through learner-learner interaction need not, nor should it, be absent from the distance education experience.

The development and growth of stable and sustaining virtual communities based upon network technologies (Turkel, 1995) supports the notion that communities can develop and thrive without physical proximity. These communities are different from their face-to-face and place-bound communities, but we cannot deny that they are meeting diverse social and intellectual needs of widely distributed individuals. Distance educators are now exploring and evaluating the potential benefits of learning communities that exist only through the mediation of telecommunications technologies. By isolating and measuring variables for quantitative analysis and engaging in rigorous qualitative investigation, researchers are gaining an understanding of the important learner-learner interaction in mediated contexts.

Audio and video teleconferencing have been shown to be capable of supporting learning communities. Anderson and Garrison (1995) identified how different learning activities and instructional design components of university courses delivered via audio teleconferencing impact the creation of these learning communities. Latchem (1995) reviews literature on video conferencing, identifying successful applications, and notes the capacity of the medium to support cultural exchange and social relationships amongst learners.

Perhaps the most exciting learning communities are being developed using computer-mediated communications systems. Harasim et al. (1995) note the characteristics of this medium to support collaborative learning (an important component of the learning community). These characteristics are the capacity for active learning, interaction (both quantity and intensity), access to group knowledge and support, democratic learning environment, convenience, and motivation to complete tasks. Collaborative experiences can be "synchronous," in which case all participants are logged onto networked computers at the same time, or "asynchronous," in which case messages or other content are left by participants in common areas for retrieval or contribution by participants when they next log-on to the network. The capacity to support interaction in an asynchronous format provides an opportunity for reflection and deliberation not found in any synchronous learning environment — including face-to-face classrooms. Learner-learner interaction on computer networks is being used to support and develop many kinds of "virtual" communities (religious, sports, professional, hobby, etc.), besides those related directly to higher education. For example, Trudy and Peter Johnson-Lenz have been supporting a "Virtual Learning Community" since 1988, in which computer-conferencing systems are used to create and sustain therapeutic relationships amongst participants (Johnson-Lenz and Johnson-Lenz, 1991).

Effective and meaningful learning communications between/among learners requires consideration of all three control dimensions (support, proficiency, and independence). First, instructional support must be provided such that meaningful learning activities are integrated with the educational goals. Instructional approaches and support must be congruent with the desired educational goal if learners are to achieve deep/meaningful learning outcomes. When communication is mediated, technological training and sustained support are imperative. Second, learning how to use the tools of communication needed to support learner-learner interaction is an issue of proficiency. Being competent users of various synchronous and asynchronous communications technologies requires considerable proficiency. Best practice dictates that higher education institutions provide opportunities for learners to gain these proficiencies — preferably in a stress-free, nongraded learning context. Finally, learner proficiency and support with regard to both content and communication skills are crucial in determining the independence associated with educational experiences at a distance. Independent learning requires considerable learning proficiency but should not be seen as an ideal. Collaborative learning experiences should not be sacrificed in the name of individual choice and freedom. Learner-learner interaction and collaborative learning enhance the quality of learning and need to be included in distance education experiences whenever practical. That is, collaborative learning activities should be included in course work and must not be seen as "optional add on" activities, but should be directly related to expected learning outcomes of the course.

The final sphere of interaction amongst participants of the educational enterprise concerns teacher-teacher interaction.

Teacher-teacher interaction

A third communication dyad looks at teacher-teacher interaction and the effects of communications technologies upon this interaction. Most professional teacher-teacher interaction takes place in a context of professional development, that is, teachers communicating with each other in order to enhance their teaching competencies. Interaction is critical to professional development (Cervero, 1990), as practitioners need to develop their learning in the applied context in which it is practiced. This professional development communication has often been confined to infrequent gatherings at face-to-face conferences or scheduled professional development seminars.

New communication tools are expanding the opportunities for teacher-teacher interaction and moving exclusive dependence upon face-to-face interaction to a distributed community which interacts "anytime/anyplace." One example of this is the e-mail distribution lists which teachers use to inform both their teaching practice and their subject matter expertise. *The Directory of Electronic Journals, Newsletters and Academic Discussion Lists*, 6th Edition, published by the Association of Research Libraries compiles listings of over 3,000 academic and professional discussion lists and 1,688 electronic journals, newsletters, and newsletter-digests. The growth of the directory indicates the explosive growth of teacher-teacher communication using this media. The 1996 edition describes an increase of 257% in journals and a 26% increase in the number of discussion lists since the 1995 edition.

Teacher-to-teacher interaction is also enhanced by the professional gatherings and conventions of teaching, learning, and academic organizations. The increasing costs and demands of time are giving rise to new forms of professional interaction known as virtual conferences (Anderson, 1996). Virtual conferences use a variety of media to support presentations and interactions among professionals in widely distributed locations. Early virtual conferences followed the presentation and discussion format common to face-to-face conferences, with dialogue being supported via e-mail (Anderson and Mason, 1993). More recently, virtual conferences have used video conferencing, virtual reality, and World Wide Web (WWW) tools to support a variety of activities, including debates, role plays, and panel discussions. Virtual conferences can be hosted at a fraction of what it would cost participants and organizers for a face-to-face conference. However, it is doubtful that the full social benefit of a relaxed face-to-face dialogue will ever be realized in a mediated context.

The issues of support, proficiency, and independence for teacher-teacher interaction are similar to those for learner-learner interaction. We next discuss the three forms of interaction, including the content dimension.

Learner-content interaction

The development of exciting new tools, which allow humans to "interact" directly with learning resources, forms the next two types of interaction leading to meaningful learning. Juler (1990) argued that "the text is the basis of all forms of education and that interactions that learners have with their texts are just as important as the interactions they have with real people" (p. 28). We disagree with the notion that interaction with content/resources carries the same potential qualitative impact as interaction with people, but we do not deny that it serves an essential function and that learning does take place through such interaction. The question is the nature and quality of such learning outcomes.

In order for meaningful interactions to occur between learner and content, the learner must actively engage the content materials. Turoff, Hiltz, and Balasubramanian (1994) describe the goals of learner-content interaction as:

- Forming degrees of agreement or disagreement with the material

- Seeking or reaching an understanding of the material

- Relating it to what one already knows (or doesn't know)

- Realizing confusions and lack of understandings that need further pursuit

They suggest the development of tools to assist learners in making explicit and public their attempts at achieving these goals. They refer to their set of tools as collaborative hypertext environments in which learners can annotate materials, create their own private and shared hypermedia links within the learning materials, and have the capacity to directly and indirectly author new items for inclusion in the database of learning resources. Thus, the record of learner-learner and learner-teacher interaction becomes the content with which succeeding learners interact.

We are just beginning to see the development of robotic support characters on the networks. Turkle (1995) documents the strange but supportive interactions between humans and software programs known as "bots" or "agents." These programs are given limited communications capacity by their creators and are designed to explain, guide, entertain, or answer queries from humans with whom they come into contact in a cyberspace environment. Educators will soon be programming bots to provide tutoring, ask questions, stimulate, and otherwise engage learners in learning conversations. Further development of intelligent tutorials, simulations, and agent-directed tutorials promises to support huge increases in both the quantity and quality of learning resources available to learners. We are just beginning to see how we can incorporate these resources into higher education programs and support learners in their effective use of these resources.

There is little doubt that the immense, eclectic, and often stimulating content available on the Internet can lead to learners and teachers spending large amounts of time exploring and learning using this medium. Like any pastime, hobby or profession, Internet use can become so time-consuming as to impact negatively other aspects of daily life. This term has been labeled "Internet addiction." A recent search using one of the Internet search engines returned 1800 sites in which the term "Internet addiction" was discussed. There are self-diagnostic instruments and even self-help groups (ironically these groups convene on the Internet) designed to help users achieve appropriate use of Internet tools. Joseph Woo maintains an interesting site (http://home.hkstar.com/~joewoo/hazard.html) which provides numerous links to the physical, psychological, and legal "dangers" of excessive Internet usage.

Distance education learners are perhaps best positioned to take advantage of new "virtual" learning resources in that they are generally more receptive to technologically mediated study and activities where face-to-face learning may not be a preferred or even a realistic possibility. The development and testing of effective virtual learning resources for distance learners could provide a competitive advantage for learner and institutions that are committed to distance education services.

It is clear from the rapid development of learning tools for use in both face-to-face and distance contexts that we are at the threshold of a renaissance of tools to support learner-content interaction. However, the increasing size of potential learning resources brought about by the growth of the Internet creates an environment that is incredibly stimulating at the same time as it can be intimidating and even addictive to learners. The key issue in this type of interaction is learner proficiency and intellectual development. Learners must have the maturity and ability to go beyond surfing the Internet and simply acquiring fragmented bits of information. Learner-content interactions on the Internet raise the question of authenticity. Research on authentic learning projects and activities (Brown et al., 1989) has shown the effectiveness of assigning learners authentic learning activities and tasks. The question is how authentic can learning experiences be, which do not consider the learner's ability to make sense of overwhelming amounts of information.

The issues raised in learner-content interaction are shared in the next dyad, teacher-content interaction.

Teacher-content interaction

Interaction between teacher and content is often subsumed as a normal component of the research or professional development function required of most teachers in formal, higher education systems. In distance education this interaction reflects the structure and flexibility of the course materials (Moore, 1989). Garrison and Shale (in Garrison, 1989) have made the argument that, in conventional higher education, transmission of content and communication generally use the same medium (e.g., lecture and questions). In traditional distance education, however, the teacher/designer prepares the lessons in a prepackaged format and closing the "communication loop is an activity separate from the transmission of information and frequently is supported by a medium different from that used to distribute the content" (p. 19). More recently, this model of distance education has been brought into question with the use of teleconferencing technologies, particularly computer conferencing, which has unified the transmission of content and communication comparable to conventional higher education.

With the increasing pace of knowledge generation within most disciplines and the impact of technological change on means and methods of communicating and accessing information, teachers have the means to interact with the learning content in many novel ways. For example, many teachers are creating WWW "home pages" as a learning resource, information repository, and promotional device for their courses. The creation of these pages provides an opportunity for the teacher to link his or her learners with the many learning resources available on the WWW. Teachers soon realize that, since their learners are being exposed to new resources and different viewpoints, knowledge is no longer containable within the teacher's classroom or the course learning package. Teachers are being exposed to the learning resources of other teachers and other institutions. This both stimulates and threatens teachers, as they realize that consumer choice and satisfaction will require them to match the variety and quality of content resources provided by competitive suppliers. The opportunity for teachers to interact with the learning content provided by other teachers is increasing dramatically as a result of the WWW. Prior to the WWW, teachers rarely or never were exposed to the means and methods by which other teachers constructed their learning content. This exposure will lead to improvements in teaching as it stimulates reflection and communication. Based upon this shared experience, teachers will be able to access and adopt the teaching content created by other teachers.

The support needed to help teachers access and organize instructional content through the WWW is very important. Teaching in a global, information-rich environment is a very different experience than lecturing in a closed classroom. Obviously new technical skills are required, but these are often the easiest to acquire. More difficult is the task of helping teachers to embrace continuous change that will mark the relationship between teachers and content for the foreseeable future. Teachers will have to cope with a world where knowledge development is continuous and where subject matter expertise is only one component of the skill set necessary to create sophisticated and effective learning content for use by learners. We do, however, see opportunities and significant progress in the development of authoring tools that assist teachers in interacting with and creating learning content. Such products as WEBCT (http://homebrew.cs.ubc.ca/webct/) and the Virtual University (http://virtual-u.cs.sfu.ca/) provide easy-to-use templates and tools that assist teachers in creating and modifying content and managing the learning environment.

Content-content interaction

Content interacting with content pushes our discussion somewhat into the realm of science fiction. Nonetheless, we are seeing early examples of programs written to retrieve information, operate other programs, make decisions, and monitor resources on the networks. These programs are known as intellegent agents (see http://www.fdc.co.uk/agent.html). For example, such an agent could be designed by an agriculture economics teacher teaching a lesson on futures marketing. The agent would regularly update the lesson examples by retrieving information from on-line future quotations and could alert the teacher or learners if any unusal activity is taking place. The lesson, thus, becomes "ever green" and gains in credibility as it displays real information from today's marketplace.

Internet search engines are other examples where intelligent agents are continuously scouring the networks and sending the results of their discoveries back to central data bases. In the not too distant future, teachers will utilize learning resources that continuously improve themselves through their interaction, not only with learners, but also with other intelligent agents.

We leave the exploration and definition of independence, proficiency, and support in the interaction of non-human learning resources to the computer scientists charged with creating and rearing these aviators!

Conclusion

Learning in a networked world presents many new roles and responsibilities for both the teacher and the learner. As well, it will radically change the construction and delivery of the course content. The issue of control will be radically challenged in higher education. The balance of control in an educational transaction mediated by technology will have to be negotiated based on the various types of interaction and will focus on issues of support, proficiency, and independence. Higher education is being transformed by new developments and applications of learning technologies both on and off campus. We believe that the use of interaction between and among learners, teachers, and content promises to increase opportunities for, and experience of, deep and meaningful learning.

However, we do not think that use of this interactive capacity within the old paradigms of learning will realize this potentiality. As Brown and Duguid (1996) state: "Without more thought to learners and their practical needs, we fear that not only will these [communication] technologies be underexploited, but they may well reinforce the current limitations of our higher education system" (p. 19). Therefore, we must reconceptualize the teaching-learning transaction in higher education if we are to fully realize the potential interactive capabilities of communication technologies and achieve higher-quality learning outcomes.

References

Anderson, T. (1994). *Socially shared cognition in distance education: An exploration of learning in an audio teleconference context.* Unpublished doctoral dissertation. University of Calgary.

Anderson, T. (1996). The Virtual Conference: Extending Professional Education in Cyberspace. *International Journal of Educational Telecommunications, 2*(2/3), 121-135.

Anderson, T., & Garrison, R. (1995). Transactional Issues in distance education: The impact of design in audioteleconferencing. *American Journal of Distance Education, 9*(2), 27-45.

Anderson, T., & Mason, R. (1993). The Bangkok Project: New tool for professional development. *American Journal of Distance Education, 7*(2), 5-18.

Brown, J. Collins, A., & Duguid, P. (1989). Situated cognition and the culture of learning. *Educational Researcher, 18*(1), 32-42.

Brown, J. S., & Duguid, P. (1996). Universities in the digital age. *Change*, July/August, 11-19.

Cervero, R. (1990). A model of professionals as learners. In R. Cervero & J. Azzaretto (Eds.). *Visions for the future of continuing professional educa - tion* (pp. 161-182). Athens, Georgia: University of Georgia.

Collins, M., & Berge, Z. (1998). Moderator's Home Page. [On-line]. Available: http://cac.psu.edu/~mauri/moderators.html

Damon, W. (1984). Peer interaction: The untapped potential. *Journal of Applied Developmental Psychology*, 5, 331-343.

Directory of electronic journals, newsletters and academic discussion lists. 6th Edition. Association of Research Libraries.

Garrison, D. R. (1989). *Understanding distance education: A framework for the future*. London: Routledge.

Garrison, D. R. (1993). An analysis of the control construct in self-directed learning. In H. B. Long (Ed.), *Emerging perspectives of self-directed learning*. Norman, OK: Oklahoma Research Center for Continuing Professional and Higher Education of the University of Oklahoma.

Garrison, D. R. (1995). Constructivism and the role of self-instructional course materials: A reply. *Distance Education*, 16(1), 136-140.

Garrison, D.R. (1997). Computer conferencing: The post-industrial age of distance education. *Open Learning* , 12(2), 3-11.

Garrison, D. R., & Baynton, M. (1987). Beyond independence in distance education: The concept of control. *The American Journal of Distance Education*, 1(3), 3-15.

Hardy, D., & Olcott, D. (1995). Audio teleconferencing and the adult Learner: Strategies for effective practice. *American Journal of Distance Education*, 9(1), 44-60.

Harasim, L., Hiltz, S., Teles, L., & Turoff, M. (1995). *Learning networks*. Cambridge Mass. MIT Press.

Johnson-Lenz, P., & Johnson-Lenz, T. (1991). Post-mechanistic groupware and primitives: Rhythms, boundaries and containers. *International Journal of Man-Machine Studies*, 34, 395-417.

Juler, P. A. (1990). Promoting interation; maintaining independence: Swallowing the mixture? *Open Learning*, 5(2), 24-33.

Latchem, C. (1995). See what I mean? Where compressed digital video conferencing works. In F. Lockwood (Ed.), *Open and distance learning today* (pp. 98-107). London: Routledge.

Lipman, M. (1991). *Thinking in education*. Cambridge: Cambridge University Press.

Moore, M. (1989). Three types of interaction. In M. Moore (Ed.), *Readings in the principles of distance education*. American Association for Distance Education. University Park: Pennsylvania State University.

Moore, M., & Kearsley, G. (1996). *Distance education: A systems view.* Belmont, CA: Wadsworth.

Oblinger, D. G., & Maruyama, M. K. (1996). *Distributed learning* (CAUSE Professional Paper Series, #14). Boulder, CO: CAUSE.

Salomon, G. (1981). *Communication and education: Social and psychologi - cal interactions*. London: Sage.

Turoff, M., Hiltz, S. R., & Balasubramanian, V. (1994). *The human element in collaborative hypertext\hypermedia*. New Jersey Institute of Technology University Heights, Newark NJ. [On-Line]. Available: http://eies.njit.edu/~turoff/Papers/cscwhy.htm

Turkel, S. (1995). *Life on the screen: Identity in the age of the Internet* . New York: Simon & Shuster.

Chapter 7

The Distance Learner in context

Chère Campbell Gibson

The Loneliness of the Long-Distance Runner — a title of a movie and a book — conjures up visions of a solitary soul running across vast plains regardless of weather. That title has been modified and one often sees reference to the loneliness of the long distance learner in the literature. Again visions of a solitary soul emerge, this time trudging to a courthouse in the middle of nowhere to sit alone in front of an audioteleconferencing convener or compressed video equipment. Or perhaps the vision emerges of an adult sitting at home alone in the eerie glow of a computer monitor in the wee hours of the morning. The contrast, of course, is the learner surrounded by ebullient peers and a doting teacher in a classroom rich with material resources. But is our distance learner in that different a situation?

As we look at the distance learner, we must remember that these learners exist in a broad social context — a social context which can profoundly affect the success of the distance teaching-learning transaction. Thus our theories of distance education must take into consideration not only the learner, teacher, content, and the communications medium (the context of education), as duly considered in a number of prevalent distance education theories (Wedemeyer, 1981; Moore, 1973; Garrison, 1989), but also this larger social context of which the learner is a part. A quick look at ecological systems theory provides a starting point for our consideration.

Ecological Systems Theory

Ecological systems theory, as outlined by Urie Bronfenbrenner (1977), draws heavily on the work of Kurt Lewin and focuses on the multiple contexts in which human development occurs.

When first published, ecological systems theory was part of a plea for psychologists to attempt to conduct more ecologically and contextually valid experimental research (Way, 1991). As Bronfenbrenner (1977) argued,

> The understanding of human development demands going beyond the direct observation of behavior on the part of one or two persons in the same place; it requires an examination of multiperson systems of interaction not limited to a single setting and must take into account aspects of the environment beyond the immediate situation containing the subject. (p. 514)

The theory is most correctly described as a transformed and extended version of the preceding Lewin (1935) formula, $b=f(PE)$. The first transformation yields $D=f(PE)$ where D represents development. Bronfenbrenner (1986) notes that the term "development" introduces a new parameter not in the earlier formulation, that of time. This seems particularly appropriate as we consider, for example, the cognitive, intellectual, personal, and social development of our dynamic distance learners over time, as exemplified by recent research findings of Herrman (1988), Powell, et. al. (1990) and others. The formula, including the time factor, is represented as:

$$D_{t-p} = f_{t-p} \, (PE)$$

where "t" refers to the time at which a developmental outcome, e.g. learning, is observed, and "t-p" to the period(s) during which the joint forces (PE) were operating over time to produce the outcome existing at the time of operation (Bronfenbrenner, 1986). What this representation allows us to consider is not only the developmental change, but also the processes that produce them. In other words, as distance educators we are interested not only in learning, but also in the interaction of those properties of the person and their multiple environments which produce constancy and change in the characteristics of that person over time.

Consider, for example, a learner's self-confidence changing over time as a result of the interaction of a growing self-awareness of his or her capabilities or acquiring excellent grades. Receiving the encouragement of others, interacting with independent learning materials which instill confidence, receiving employer rewards of more sophisticated job assignments as a result of new academic pursuits, and perceiving peers' and family's new-found pride in our learner's success, are just some of the examples of how one might enhance learner's self-confidence.

Microsystem

In his early writings Bronfenbrenner (1977) suggests that the ecological environment be conceived topologically as a nested arrangement of structures, each contained within the next. He further describes the four systems within the total system. The first of these systems is the Bronfenbrenner microsystem, defined as the complex of relationships between the developing person and environment in an immediate setting containing that person (Bronfenbrenner, 1977). This is our distance learner as student or as worker or family member, even community member. Place, time, physical features, activity, participant, and role constitute the elements of setting in ecological theory. In the 1980s Bronfenbrenner modified his definition of the microsystem to include consideration of the personal characteristics of others in the environment recognizing the potential impact of the other person's temperament, personality, and systems of belief.

Mesosystem

Bronfenbrenner's mesosystem comprises the interrelations among major settings containing the developing person at a particular point in his or her own life — in essence the mesosystem is a system of microsystems. For our distance learner the mesosystem encompasses the interactions among the distance learning institution, the family, the workplace, the community, and perhaps a religious institution, and other contexts unmentioned.

Exosystems

Further, Bronfenbrenner (1977) suggests that, in addition to the microsystems and mesosystem, one needs to be cognizant of those other social structures, both formal and informal, which, although they may not contain the individual, "impinge upon or encompass the immediate settings in which that person is found, and thereby influence, delimit or even determine what goes on there" (Bronfenbrenner, 1977, p. 515). Structures which may be considered as part of this exosystem include: the neighborhood, the mass media, the world of work, agencies of government at all levels, communications and transportation systems, the distribution of goods and services, and informal social networks.

Macrosystem

Lastly one must consider the macrosystem, which differs in a fundamental way from the preceding systems. Rather than referring to specific contexts that affect the life of the person, the macrosystem refers to the "overarching institutional patterns of the culture or subculture, such as economic, social, educational, legal and political systems of which micro-, meso- and exosystems are the concrete manifestations" (Bronfenbrenner, 1977, p. 515). Additionally, Bronfenbrenner refers to these macrosystems as blueprints that provide patterns. One example he provides is the school classroom, which in any given society looks very much alike. This similarity is found in other settings and institutions as well, both formal and informal. In some cases, laws, regulations, and rules provide the blueprint. In other instances the blueprints are more informal and implicit and manifest in custom, tradition, and practice of everyday life. As Bronfenbrenner (1986) notes, we need to give particular attention to "the developmentally instigating belief systems, resources, hazards, life styles, opportunity structures, life course options, and patterns of social interaction that are imbedded in each of these systems (micro-, meso- and exosystems)" (p. 228).

Throughout we must remain mindful that the context, both proximal and remote, can invite, permit, or inhibit progressive development over time in interaction with the individual's characteristics which encourage or discourage interactions with that environment. Overall, Bronfenbrenner's ecological systems theory helps us go beyond the conception of a decontextualized or single-context learner to recognizing the learner in multiple contexts at a specific point in time in sociohistory.

Figure 1, adapted from Egan and Cowan (1979, p. 116), provides a pictoral look at the individual in his or her multiple contexts.

Further, Bronfenbrenner (1986) reminds us of Vygotsky's (1978) thesis that individual development is defined and delimited by the possibilities available to it in a given culture or subculture at a given point in time in history. Further he notes that the context in which cognition takes place is not simply an adjunct to the cognition, but a constituent of it (Ceci,

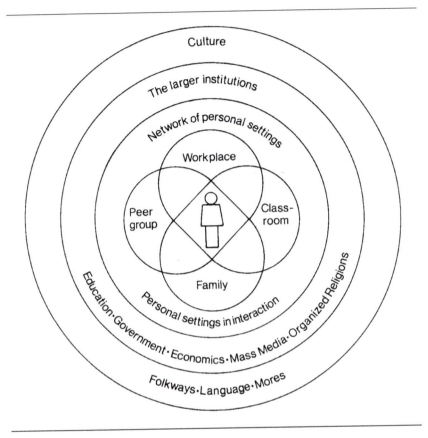

Figure 1: The Individual in Multiple Contexts
(adapted from Egan and Cowan, 1979)

Bronfenbrenner and Baker, 1988, p. 243). Let's look more closely and 'listen' to the words of distance learners as they reflect on their life in context (Gibson and Graff, 1992; Graff and Coggins, 1989).

Emerging Influential Factors

At the microsystem level, we hear learners describe their world of work, as full- or part-time workers within or outside of the home, with varying levels of responsibility in routine or chaotic employment situations. For some work hours vary, others are on call a large percentage of the time. A sense of confidence or command is evident. Our learners are also found at home, where they may live as single individuals, often with pets and/or significant others in their lives. The majority are found in nuclear families with children of varying ages.

Many are active in their community, playing valuable roles as literacy tutors, city council representatives, and members of parent-teacher groups. Many distance learners are reluctant to give up these rewarding civic activities. On a lighter note, we find our learners in leisure roles, e.g. as volleyball team members and home talent baseball players.

As learners they focus their discussion on the processes and content of learning at a distance. Early in their studies they describe their percep-tions of themselves as learners in adulthood with a focus on their abilities to learn. Further, they consider their abilities to learn at a distance, including their perceived ability to self-manage, their powers of self-discipline, their love of learning and of reading, and the strength of their motivation. Positive and negative images abound as they question their abilities. So too as they describe their goals for learning, questioning whether or not they are realistic, given their abilities in certain subject matter areas, a lack of understanding of faculty expectations, and a concern for their availability. What's striking in the initial three to four months is the generally poor academic self-concept in sharp contrast to the positive general self-concept, evident in their descriptions of them-selves in other contexts. The extent to which they can resolve these perceptions and concerns positively appears critical, particularly relative to their self-concept as a learner (Gibson, 1996).

As we begin to focus our attention on the interaction among and between those microsystems that contain the individual learner, we begin to see a variety of additional forces which could potentially enhance or inhibit learning. These forces go beyond those which are unique to the learner as he/she relates to the distance teaching institution, faculty, content, and the related technology. As school and family microsystems begin to interact, we find the learner striving to positively resolve concerns of self-management, especially time and energy, to establish priorities, and to find a balance between the learner's own needs for study time and the needs of home and family. Others within the environment contribute either positively or negatively to the resolution of these challenges in terms of their support.

Support appears to be multifaceted, and includes emotional, logistical, economical, and educational support. Emotional support includes expres-sions of pride and encouragement in contrast to questioning the appro-priateness of the pursuit. Logistical support includes, for example, creating a space for learning, quiet times, and sharing household chores and responsibilities, in contrast to requesting the learner take fewer classes in order to continue all pre-enrollment family obligations. Working multiple jobs on the part of a significant other versus requesting the learner pursue a second job to pay for the cost of tuition provides an example of varying degrees of economical support. Contrast these positive examples of educational support — sons (college students themselves) share books and tutor Mom in math, husband serves as sounding board for new knowledge — with a progress inhibiting behavior, that of not taking the learner's pursuit seriously.

When the learner's world of school intersects with the world of work, other forces emerge. Once again we find the learner struggling with time and energy management, coupled with the stress of trying to ensure everything gets done at work as well as at school. Often the learner finds himself or herself weighing the value of a promotion versus rapidity of degree completion. Motivation also looms — external motivation when the degree is required to maintain current employment or the internal motivation of voluntarily recareering when the degree is complete.

Multifaceted support emerges once again. Examples of emotional support include encouragement from co-workers and boss and others, signaling concurrence with the learner's course of action, in contrast to co-workers who become abrasive and appear threatened by the learner's return to school. Time away from work and flexible hours permitted for educational requirements versus frequent shift changes and required overtime provide examples of enhancing and inhibiting environmental forces of a logistical support nature. Payment of tuition or other monetary incentives provide a positive economic display of support, with empathetic mentoring by a supervisor providing a source of educational support. The absence of either also sends a signal, albeit negative.

Learners also describe a circle of friends as another context separate from a community context. Learners continue to struggle with time, energy, stress management and the setting of priorities. The circle of friends often becomes smaller with the intersection of other microsystems, especially family and work coupled with school. This diminishing circle, however, provides varying levels of its share of support. While the data reported here failed to uncover instances of economic support, there were examples of emotional support — through direct expressions of support and empathy from those who are also in school — and logistical support, for example, picking up required books on campus for a fellow student.

Educational support included friends who had completed degrees providing tutoring to a friend still pursuing one. Negative forces emanating from the learner's circle of friends appear infrequent, perhaps because these 'friends' were among those dropped from the circle of acquaintances.

As we listen to our learners consider their lives in the community, we hear reluctance expressed relative to diminishing their community involvement as tutors, councilpersons, church choir members, etc. Yet some recognize the need to set priorities, adjusting and/or dropping certain community activities, and replacing the time spent with studies. While the community and related leisure provide a pull away from studies, the community also provides an environment to test goals and new knowledge, as many noted.

Overall, as we look at the mesosystems, the distance learners noted the existence and the need to have another life in addition to school, as well as the importance of being able to balance these various lives. What's striking is the growing ability that emerged over time to set realistic time frames, to establish a routine for studies, and to rearrange priorities. Seasonal challenges were still noted, for example, fine summer weather, holidays, etc., but these were being accounted for with increased frequency in advanced planning. What is perhaps less striking is the impact of the learner and his or her educational pursuits on those that surround them; in learning in context the learner impacts the context itself — an exciting dynamic.

As we look at the forces that exist in the exosystem of our learner's life, few factors emerge, but those forces identified are quite critical — costs. These costs include the rising cost of tuition, which begins to deny access to many, regardless of delivery mechanisms employed. Couple this with the cost of purchasing expensive textbooks, frequently reprinted in new editions to discourage the secondary purchase market, laws which penalize distance learners in terms of financial aid awards, the unequal distribution of wealth, and the cost of education becomes insurmountable for some and requires irregular enrollment by others.

As we consider macrosystem forces, those 'blueprints' in our lives, we see a new blueprint for education emerging, one which includes distance education, a positive force in the lives of our distance learners. But not all have seen or have come to appreciate the new model of education and our learners hear others question the value of such education, raising doubts in the learner's mind. Other traditional values and beliefs also provide negative forces to impede progress. These include a questioning of the appropriateness: of women pursuing postsecondary education, of husbands in schools while wives work, of older persons (beyond the traditional age of 21) enrolled in degree programs, and men and women alike considering recareering in their 30s and 40s. Some of our learners struggle with the same concerns of appropriateness. Overall, while our learners voice an understanding that 'education serves as a vehicle to open up new venues and provide increased choice,' emotional support and often related logistic, economic, and educational support is denied by others, impeding progress.

Learning in Context

Thus we begin to see a pattern of individual learners engaging, to a greater or lesser extent, in an attempt to evoke a response from, alter, or create an external environment for learning. Maintaining internal motivation and a sense of self-efficacy and balance is a concurrent challenge. But remember too that each member of a microsystem influences every other member. Our challenge as researchers is to begin to better understand learners in context and the impact of their learning, both positively and negatively, on those who share their lives in the multiple interacting contexts that contain them. Our challenge as educators is to consider how the context might be seen as a partner in teaching and learner support. But where do we start?

Interventions in a single course

Perhaps it's easiest to consider our own courses as a starting point. How might we rethink our educational offerings in light of the fact we have a distance learner learning in context? In some instances it's easy. Those teaching in baccalaureate degree completion programs in nursing have long encouraged their distance learners to practice newfound skills and theories on the hospital wards and in the clinics where they are employed daily. But what about those whose course work and employment seem less connected? Let's first examine our basic assignments — to what extent do our course assignments allow a learner to select a learning experience, within the boundaries of the course, that reflects his or her interests and goals for taking the courses, etc.? For example, to what extent can the policewoman assigned to a community beat and pursuing a communications course select an option which permits her to test a variety of communications strategies on her beat and report her findings? Her job is to enhance communications between her community members and the police force. Surely a communications course would help her do that! Yes, regardless of assignments she should be able to enhance communications within the community, but wouldn't it seem a win-win situation if an application assignment could be developed that would facilitate a move from theory to practice? In this real-life example, no such assignment option existed.

Not only is the environment a rich resource for conducting assignments, it's also a rich resource for conducting learning. We often worry about the distance learner and his or her separation from the teacher, yet we forget teachers surround the learner. Consider the bank teller working on a Bachelor of Business Administration struggling with accounting. Separated from the teacher, perhaps, but not from accountants. Accountants surround him or her! We need to empower the learner to assess their context for resources and to seek out those resources as another source of help. Empowered learners describe high school seniors tutoring them in introduction to college math, former high school teachers providing chemistry tips, work colleagues lending an ear to discuss the application of a new management concept in the world of work, water treatment plant employees helping with ecology experiments. Small community librarians continually emerge as nominees for sainthood by distance learners. No one seems better able or more willing to seek out learning resources, print- or Internet-based. Distance educators have come to understand and appreciate the value of peers. In distance education delivery systems, which require that learners come to one or more sites, courses are designed with application exercises to encourage peer interaction and sharing onsite. The result — educational and emotional supports, and often even logistical support. Similar small group work can be encouraged in the online environment. The challenge is perhaps greatest when learners are involved in individualized self-paced programs at a distance, but even then educators have discovered distance learners are willing to share their names and phone numbers and willingly chat and even meet with 'class-mates' to provide support. What's key is that this important interaction is built into course planning.

Increasingly we are seeing courses offered at a distance to other distance classrooms that may include a corporate board room (or lunch room more frequently!). Examples include foreign language classes and engineering courses. To what extent can this site be used a source of case studies, real-life examples, resources to be added to the class?

As we talk of the importance of linking theory to practice, as education increasingly focuses on active learning, situated cognition, and authentic assessment, our distance learner is perfectly positioned. Can we take advantage of this situation and encourage active learning in context as we look at our own course design, required assignments, suggested resources, etc.?

Interventions in degree programs

For those who not only offer a variety of courses at a distance, but also offer full degree programs, other strategies might be considered to encourage further support from the distance learner's context. One example is that of a baccalaureate degree program at a distance which conducts a new student orientation. Not a new idea, but it takes on a new twist when the orientation is conducted for a day for the entire family. The purpose is to help the entire family examine the new adventure, its benefits and challenges, and how, as a family unit, they can be successful. Graduates share their stories of successful graduation, of children doing homework with parents and of strategies to ensure progress toward degree yet maintain quality family time.

Recognition of employers and other community resources who supported our new graduates throughout their studies is yet another way to encourage continual involvement of resources that surround our learners.

Policy interventions

To the solitary educator, it seems less clear how one might intervene in the larger arena where policies and procedures exist which disadvantage our distance learners. Financial aid policies, which discriminate against distance learners, especially part-time distance learners, are an example. In addition, strict residency rules and differential treatment of courses taken off campus may be a reality at your institution, further disadvantaging the distance learner. Can you help? Probably. Just by understanding your distance learners, who they are, and why they are pursuing their degrees at a distance. Have an understanding of their progress and success and being able to share that with others is a start. Helping colleagues put a face to the distance learner motivates others to reconsider policies of old with rationales long gone and provides concrete examples for consideration.

Conclusions

Questions abound and answers are scarce. As Kember et al. (1994) note, "Student services are most likely to be successful if their objectives are to assist students with the process of integrating study into work, family and social demands ... area(s) over which the college has limited influence" (p. 299-300). Perhaps our greatest service is to begin to understand the existence and impact of multiple forces, so as to create awareness and provide a source of emotional support to learners as they begin to act upon their multiple contexts toward the end of achieving their learning goals.

References

Bronfenbrenner, U. (1977). Toward an experimental ecology of human development. *American Psychologist*, 7, 513-531.

Bronfenbrenner, U. (1986). Ecological systems theory. *Annuals of Child Development* 6, 187-249.

Ceci, S., Bronfenbrenner U., & Baker, J. (1988). Memory in context: The case of prospective memory. In F. Weinert & M. Perlmutter (Eds.) *Universals and changes in memory development* (p. 243-256). Hillsdale, NJ: Lawrence Erlbaum.

Egan, G. & Cowan , M. (1979). *People in systems: A model for development in the human-services professions and education.* Monterey, CA: Brooks-Cole Publishing Co.

Garrison, D. R. (1989). *Understanding distance education: A framework for the future.* New York: Routledge.

Gibson, C. (1996). Academic self-concept: Its nature and import in distance education. *American Journal of Distance Education* 10(1), 23-36.

Gibson, C. & Graff, A.. 1992. Impact of adult's preferred learning styles and perception of barriers on completion of external baccalaureate degree programs. *Journal of Distance Education,* VII(1), 39-51.

Graff A. & C. Coggins. 1989. Twenty voices. In *Proceedings Adult Education Research Conference.* Madison, Wisconsin: University of Wisconsin-Madison, pp. 159-164.

Herrman, A. (1988). A conceptual framework for understanding the transitions in perceptions of external students. *Distance Education,* 9(1), 1-26.

Kember, D, Lai, T., Murphy, D, Siaw, I, & K.S. Yuen. (1994) Student progress in distance education courses: A replication study. *Adult Education Quarterly* 45(1), 286-301.

Lewin, K. (1935). *Dynamic theory of personality.* New York: McGraw-Hill.

Moore, M. (1973) Toward a theory of independent learning and teaching. *Journal of Higher Education*, 44, 661-679.

Powell, R., Conway, C., & Ross, L.. (1990). Effects of students' predisposing characteristics on students' success. *Journal of Distance Education*, V(1), 5-19.

Vygotsky, L. (1978) *Mind in society*. Cambridge, MA: Harvard University Press.

Wedemeyer, C. (1981) *Learning at the back door*. Madison, WI: University of Wisconsin Press.

Chapter 8

Supporting learners at a distance from inquiry through completion

Daniel Granger and Meg Benke

A staff member at a university learning technology center happily notified me that the center had just completed a new computer-interactive writing course using hypertext. Students would receive immediate formative feedback on their writing exercises as they worked through the course.

"This will be great for distance learners," she beamed.

"Sounds really good," I said. "What's the platform?"

"Macintosh."

"But most working adults only have easy access to PC's. What about them?"

"Well, they can use our computer labs."

"Oh. From Nova Scotia?"

The overarching lesson for every aspect of distance learner support is: *Know your learners.* Know who they are, where they are, and what's available to them. Understand their needs and limitations in regard to every aspect of your program. Providing real access to education at a distance involves ensuring that your intended learners can be successful in your program. The Education Network of Maine asks, "What happens to Amy?" (their typical distance learner) whenever they consider changes and new developments. In this chapter, we will spell out what that means in major program areas and provide some examples and case studies.

Marketing experts tell us that every aspect of the product, program, or service is a marketing activity, building client satisfaction and loyalty to ensure repeat business (or not). Similarly, successful student support is a result of every aspect of a program, from a prospective student's first awareness of the program to graduation day, working in an integrated fashion to maintain the student's engagement and progress. Students find programs supportive not because there is a Coordinator of Student Support available from 9 to 3 to solve their problems, but because the program was designed with the student perspective in mind by faculty and staff who understand that distance learners need and expect a responsive program.

Understanding distance learners sounds simple enough when we consider how we are able to understand our traditional students. But distance learners are 1) not around to talk to and 2) will not stick around if the program does not work for them. In thinking about how to raise real awareness and sensitivity to distance learners, it is important to understand the assumptions and inclinations faculty and staff already have. Distance learning programs vary not only in size but in their relation to other programs within the same institution. Few originated as distance education programs. Some distance learning programs began from an engineering school's interest in using new technologies; some are an outgrowth of an existing adult education program; still others originated in the outreach and extension missions of university continuing education programs. In each case, there is an existing inclination and infrastructure which must be reckoned with. And in each case, an understanding of the learner's profile can provide an invaluable prism through which to view its effectiveness.

From initial program and course design, through promotion, intake, registrarial logistics, and the delivery of courses, faculty and staff must be aware of their prospective students' circumstances and needs. This is notably a problem when campus programs seek to serve distance learners. A delivery technology is selected, but too frequently the attendant operations and supports are provided as afterthoughts. *Know your learners.* Where are they? How and when do they access your programs? What can go wrong to interrupt the program personally or technically? A program serving a cross-town site through microwave has different concerns from one serving students nationally or internationally using the Internet. Professional, technical, and clerical staff as well as faculty must each take into account learner characteristics and needs to contribute to a successful program.

Who Are Your Learners?

The majority of distance learners are adults beyond the traditional age of undergraduate college attendance. They are returning to education usually for an identifiable reason: to qualify for promotion, to prepare for a new job, because their employer expects it, or even because it's something they now want to finish. In many cases, returning learners are goal oriented (e.g., gaining the degree or certificate) more than task-oriented (anticipating the actual study and learning process). Distance learners usually have busy lives already, and education must compete with jobs, childcare, household responsibilities, etc. Whether your program is open to a broad range of participants or is targeted to a specific population within an organization, it is important to know that rarely will your program have students' undivided attention.

Beyond these general observations, successful distance educators understand the particular characteristics of the students they wish to serve. The program and supports, as well as all marketing and promotion, begin with this understanding. Broad areas of understanding of prospective students include:

Knowledge

What are the knowledge goals of the program and what knowledge do the prospective students have? It is important to build on what students actually know. In some cases, assessment pretests are valuable to both the student and the provider institution. The British Open University provides self-assessment tests to help students determine if they need preparatory work before undertaking particular courses.

Prior Skills

What are the skills required to be successful in the program and what skills do the prospective students actually have? Academic skills include critical reading, writing, and quantitative skills, but equally important are skills in time management, information retrieval, and study habits.

Experience

What experience does the program assume and what experiences are prospective students likely to bring to the program? This can be as broad as communicating effectively at a distance and as specific as using a particular software application on the computer. It is not uncommon for adult distance learners to have significant experience in a narrow aspect of a field, especially practical experience. It is often important that the program is designed to accommodate these background differentials.

Culture

What cultural background does the program assume and what backgrounds do the prospective students actually have? This can of course refer to obvious cultural (and linguistic) differences, but subtler differences must also be recognized, especially as programs cross regional and even national boundaries. This becomes very important when the application of abstract principles can result in quite different practices and outcomes.

Context

What context does the program expect for the learners and what context do they actually inhabit? Computer availability is only one example; the order, time, and opportunity to undertake various kinds of assignments or research can be a critical factor.

Goals and motivations

What does the program assume about the learners' goals and motivations and what is actually known about them? Joy in the pursuit of learning and knowledge for its own sake are noble, but usually not sufficient to bring busy adults back to the time and expense of formal learning. To know why someone is in a program and what outcomes she or he expects can provide a valuable tool in supporting (and retaining) that student.

Learning patterns and styles

What teaching and learning approach does the program use and what learning approach is most successful for the learners? The recent emphasis on active learning and the importance of building interactive activities into programs has moved us much beyond the passive learning lecture-presentation of the past. Educators continue to explore flexible modes which can support different ways of knowing and learning. Computer-based multimedia programs show much promise here.

How Do You Support Their Decision to Return to Education?

From the moment a perspective student learns of your program, there will be decision points for him or her at each one of which you win or lose an enrollment. Traditional "marketing" talks about product (the content and format of the program), price, and performance. Certainly each of these will be a positive or negative feature for prospective students. But even in the first contact, there are positive steps of support. Prospective students are turned off by:

- A phone receptionist "too busy" or without the resources to provide full information

- A phone receptionist so intent on getting information for the marketing database that the inquirer can't get her or his questions answered

- A two- or three-week delay in receiving program information

- No ready way to get further information and counseling

The time and resources invested at the outset to respond to and engage inquiries effectively can serve not only to improve enrollments, but to provide an important information base for the continuing success and retention of enrolled students. This is true for individual students, and especially for targeted populations of students with shared characteristics or experiences.

Many successful programs have established processes of assessment in which they determine the learning profile and needs of prospective students at the outset of the program. For specific populations, broad characteristics can be determined through various means, including self- or organizational description (e.g., by Human Resources), survey instruments, and focus groups. The point of these is to understand enough about the learner's circumstances and learning needs that some element of the program does not present a barrier to successful study. This will also assist your promotional and marketing activities.

For instance, suppose your learning and technology center offers to add an interactive inquiry system to your World Wide Web site. This can enable inquiring students to enter their field of interest and preferred mode of study in order to receive an individualized report on what the program offers them. However, the majority of your students are in Human Services, and your recent survey indicated that most of them only use computers in their offices, and that fewer than 10% have ever used the Internet. Is it worth the investment?

Focus groups with prospective students and their sponsors can help to ascertain student needs and to make the best match with institutional resources. Investing in this type of analysis allows for the design of services which can help to make students successful.

Summary

Know your learners: Anticipate their concerns and provide support in the program design. Be ready and able to provide information when and as they need it. Marketing databases are only as good as your ability to respond to the learners.

How Do You Prepare Them to Be Successful Learners?

Gatekeeping vs. shepherding

Traditionally, admissions processes played a gatekeeping function, filtering applications to admit only those who fit the institution's or program's preferred profile. Those who passed through the filter presumably had the requisite preparation to succeed in the program. The premise of distance learning is at 180 degrees from this: distance learning is designed to accommodate the needs of the learner by providing learning opportunities accessible to him or her. Consequently, it is important to know what improves accessibility. Successful distance learning programs use counseling and academic advising to ensure learner success.

Portfolios

Good counseling can be combined with a student portfolio which documents the learner's needs, interests, and prior learning. Thus after learners have determined through initial academic advice that the program offers what they seek, counseling and detailed academic advising can ensure a good fit. Prior learning assessment is conducted at a distance by institutions such as Ohio University, University of Maryland, and Empire State College, and is usually integrated into a college course.

Orientations

A number of programs, recognizing that their adult students have been away from formal study for some period, provide a full orientation program to prepare them for their new study activities. This "Returning to Learning" activity can take various forms, from a face-to-face weekend session on campus to a term-long credit-bearing study of adult learning strategies. Organization, time-management, and study skills are critical components. Peer learners can be valuable for cooperative learning, simulations, team activities, and simply staying on track.

The University of Maine has developed a series of videotapes which are broadcast through its telecourse system (Dexter and Kane, 1995) and Rochester Institute of Technology and Empire State College have developed and distribute videotapes. Topics are directed to support the learner in areas such as distance learning success, writing, independent study, stress reduction, time management, and career options.

Study skills resources typical in campus environments are also important to distance learners. If print and phone are the major approaches to learning, resources should be available via this format. The University of Maryland, University College has setup study skills assistance via the phone. Empire State College has setup a virtual writing center on the Web. A key component of this service, however, is a phone number with voice mailbox for individual tutorial support for those who do not have access to the Web.

Career and counseling support is now also available through mentors and advisors with the addition of print resources, videos, and electronic resources. Current career information through the Internet is easily accessible through the gophers and Web sites for networking, résumé and employee services, job lines, and assessment. Colleges such as Appalachian State University have created on-line counseling centers to provide standard information and to answer questions.

What Learner Supports Are Built into the Delivery of the Program?

Organizations which deliver distance learning must be adaptive to learners, needs and student support services must reflect the unique goals of students outlined in the previous sections. Even the perfect CD-ROM or course guide will fail if the student does not receive good instructions or get them on time. These are some suggestions for delivery:

A. *Keep administrative processes simple, convenient, and automatic.* Standardize the processes for communication and offer provisions for communications through fax, phone, mail, computers, and other electronic means.

B. *Make both self-help strategies and direct assistance available to aid learners in solving problems as they are encountered.* All staff should be trained in support service resources and recognize that they have a responsibility to address concerns of students. But programs should be designed so that learners can help themselves, since they often study at non-office times. Use phone or electronic options for students to get questions answered or to leave a message and get a prompt reply. Fax-on-Demand services or self-help booklets might help a student through a rough spot.

C. *Provide back-up materials and systems.* Make provisions for alternate arrangements if you know that there is a possibility that a course guide will not be available. Students participating in a telecourse should have clear instructions about what to do if the instructor does not show up. Realize that there will be expectations or problems, but analyze your program and policies once you have multiple situations or exceptions.

D. *Continually learn from your experience as an organization.* A good test is to walk through your systems as a learner to see if they are easy and convenient to use. Ask for feedback on administrative strengths and shortcomings and ask support staff to report on concerns.

What Learner Supports Are Built into the Academic Program to Build Motivation and Confidence?

One way to enhance the motivation and confidence of the student is to build on the relevant experiences in which the student has been successful — usually tied to work or home. Each study activity should be designed so that the student can articulate his or her goals, including how his or her past experience can contribute to goals. If content in the courses can be built on real-life examples, learners will be more successful. In addition, every course must have clear instructions. The worst situation for a distant student is to have carved out time to work and not understand what is expected. If you structure your learning materials and student service guides in similar packages or formats, it helps the learner to learn an approach to study. If site-based study centers are an option, they should be accessible and easy to use, with on site support or referral available.

In programs in which students come together for short periods (telecourses or videocourses) or residency-based programs, every opportunity should be taken to enhance the community for the learners. Of course, technical support and process facilitation are important. But even more important is the student service support to help students to create a learning community. Peer support networks and mentoring help to promote student success. The National Technological University (NTU) provides engineering courses through a video and satellite network (Oliveira, et al., 1989). Site coordinators provide support for the infrastructure, administration, tutoring, feedback, and facilitate local activities.

How Do Faculty Support Distance Learners?

Successful distance learning programs are learning organizations, which grow, adapt, and change based on the needs of the learners served. Part of this learning process is promoting effective faculty involvement in program design and delivery and supporting faculty development. A distance learning program must provide student supports which go beyond the delivery of courses; however, the faculty who teach the courses often provide the integrative function of linking the academic program and the student to academic and support services. Unlike conventional campus programs, a faculty member cannot send the student to the Deans Office for information. The faculty for distance learners must be aware of resources for students and be willing to make referrals. It may at times go in the other direction: the faculty may become the whole college for the student. Distance learning programs must be designed to support faculty teaching at a distance.

Faculty should be trained and evaluated in methods of effective distance instruction. Distance learners need knowledge of assignments in advance, structure, and prompt feedback. Any instructional program is only as good as its ability to connect with its students. Program administrators should work with faculty to adapt instruction to the learner profile. The experiences, goals, and expectations of the learners should be integrated into the learning activity. Helping faculty to assess expectations and skills of distance learners through administrative and support services will assist students in the courses.

In order to deliver the courses, a faculty member must be at least somewhat proficient with the technology or have access to student support services. Effective use of technology in distance learning requires an ability to visualize the potential of expanding opportunities for students. The New School in New York and Empire State College have both received funding from the Sloan Foundation to provide faculty development to develop on-line courses.

Faculty at Empire State College teaching courses via computer conferencing routinely set up chat rooms for more informal student interaction. When technical employees enrolled in a course wanted to talk more about how examples applied to a particular work setting, a special chat room was set-up. Faculty must have support and input into delivery issues.

Summary

The *Guiding Principles for Distance Learning in a Learning Society*, intended to provide guidance and support for all educators and trainers using distance learning methods, address their second principle to learner support: "Distance learning opportunities are effectively supported for learners through fully accessible modes of delivery and resources." Each organization providing distance learning has the responsibility to assist learners in effectively using the resources provided through a learning support system (ACE, 1996). In this chapter we have tried to suggest strategies for providing that support.

NOTE: Further explication of some of the ideas expressed here is available through the University of Wisconsin module *Learner Support Services*, part of the distance learning certificate program.

References

American Council on Education (1996). *Guiding principles for distance learning in a learning society*. Washington, DC: ACE Central Services.

Dexter, K., & Kane K. (1995). *Preparing for distance learning: How should student affairs respond?* American College Personnel Conference —

Transforming the Academy: New perspectives and practices in higher education, Boston, MA.

Geith, G., and Foore, V. (1991). *Teaching how to learn at a distance: A solution for orienting new students*. Designing for Learner Access: Challenges and Practices in Distance Education, proceedings of the seventh conference on distance teaching and learning, Madison, WI, 196-199.

Oliveira, J. B., Fwu, B., Livingston, R., Skewes-Cox, T., & Vanderkelen, B. (1990). *The national technological university: The receiving end.* In F. LeFevre & B. van Muylwijk (eds.) Training for Competitiveness, proceedings of the European Training Technology Event, pp. 187-200.

In retrospect

Chère Campbell Gibson

So, when it's all said and done, what does all this mean to those of us who'll enter the distance education classroom tomorrow? To those who are about to teach at a distance next semester? To those who are still debating whether or not to jump into the fray? Does it mean we can no longer do business as usual? Maybe and maybe not.

The message that seems to be conveyed by the authors is that we, as distance educators, need to be learner-centered reflective practitioners. Echoing this sentiment in part, the American Council on Education (1996), in its publication entitled *Guiding Principles for Distance Learning in a Learning Society*, notes, "The diversity of learners, learning needs, learning contexts and modes of learning must be recognized if the learning activities are to achieve their goals" (p. 11). We must ask ourselves to what extent our programs are responding thoughtfully to this diversity. How are we supporting our learners through their studies at a distance? Are we setting up our learners to be successful? Let's review a summary of 'best practices' for learner support, as suggested by our authors, asking questions about our own existing or proposed distance education programs.

Know the Learner

There is really no other place to start. Who are the learners in our programs? Who do we hope to serve in the future? Thompson reminds us that distance learners are a dynamic and heterogeneous group. With diversity in age, gender, culture, and disability, no single general profile will fit. These learners also vary greatly in their past educational and life experiences, their preferred ways of learning, their knowledge and understanding of technology, and their experience learning at a distance through technology. They come to each learning experience with differing learning goals and resources, e.g., economic or emotional support, to achieve them.

We need to develop a profile of each learner in our program through written surveys, interviews, and the like. We need to discover this diversity so we can recognize it and design programs to capitalize on it. But the survey can serve several purposes. While the institution or the individual faculty member comes to better understand the learners, the learners come to better understand themselves. Questions that ask learners to identify their learning goals and objectives foster mental and emotional involvement in their studies. The identification of the barriers and enhancers to achieving these goals helps learners develop plans for time and stress management and the use of resources in their family, community, place of work, etc. Instruments that allow learners to assess their learning styles enables learners to make plans in terms of the learning strategies that will enable them to succeed.

Provide Orientations

Learners need to be oriented at several levels. To be successful, the learner needs more than an orientation to the campus, particularly when he or she might never set foot on it again until graduation. Learners, particularly returning adults, benefit from an orientation to learning in higher education and the related expectations that enable them to be strategic in their learning, to self-monitor, and engage in self-regulation activities to enhance their learning success. Our learners also need an orientation to learning at a distance with its new roles and responsibilities for teachers and learners alike. Time and stress management might also be included, as well as activities to encourage learners to develop study plans that include decisions about both the time and the effort to devote to their studies. Learners also need an orientation to the technologies they will use in individual classes and the sources of help, should they need it!

It's interesting to note that a number of institutions extend invitations to orientation programs beyond the learner to include family members young and old, recognizing the importance of the family support in learner success. Employers are even asked to sign pledges specifying that they support the learner, not only economically and emotionally, but also through the allocation or work time to be devoted to the employee's studies. Once again, the strategies used need to consider the learner and his or her specific life situation, as well as the institution and its capabilities and constraints.

Orientations of sort need to be embedded in individual course materials as well. Distance learners need to understand the faculty member's expectations for the course and their performance in it. Examples and exemplars are particularly helpful. Additionally, learning guidance that is subject-specific enables learners to progress with greater self-assurance of success. To what extent do we provide these orientations currently?

Design with Variety, Active Engagement, and Choice

As we design learning experience, we need to ask ourselves, are we enabling a variety of learning styles to coexist? Multiple modes and media can be used to present the same content in different ways. Have we selected a variety of learning resources and learning tasks relevant to the diverse life experiences and contexts of our learners? If our learners have been encouraged to establish personal learning goals, have we designed a learning environment that enables learners to pursue these goals, with meaningful instructional activities and flexibility in assignments that are integrated with the learner's personal goals? This requires a delicate and dynamic balance of attention to the teacher, learner, and content, as well as their context.

If collaborative learning experiences enhance the quality of learning and foster the use of higher-order thinking skills, to what extent have we designed learning environments that encourage and enable high levels of interaction among and between teachers, learners, content, and context? If it is important to help learners challenge their current mental frameworks, to examine value systems, and to see problem-solving and critical thinking modeled by others, have we designed learning environments that enable these activities? To what extent have we incorporated their context as a learning resource to ground their learning in their daily reality?

We also need to ask ourselves if we are supporting our distance learners' development of proficiencies as learners of a body of knowledge. To what extent have we embedded learner support devices in the instructional materials? Have we modeled approaches to learning in our interactions with them? Again, we face a delicate balancing act, this time among and between learner independence, support, and proficiency.

And perhaps last, but not least, if our learners have questions about the content or an assignment, about the technology they're using for class or about a learning process, where do they turn? And can they access this help outside of the normal work hours and through a variety of modes, e.g., phone, electronic mail, etc.?

Evaluate Authentically

Learners want to know if they are succeeding in their studies. Hopefully our learners are monitoring their own progress and adjusting the time and effort devoted to their studies accordingly. But we can make the a process easier. We can embed self-assessment tools in the instructional materials to enable the learners to determine the extent to which they can understand and apply the content. In addition to facilitating self-assessment, many would suggest that we evaluate frequently and provide considerable feedback.

Not only should we ask ourselves if we are facilitating both self-assessment and frequent faculty assessment, we need to examine the nature of the assessment. Are we encouraging the use of authentic assessment in our courses, including case studies, portfolio development, interviews, and projects emerging from the learner's context to enhance situated learning? To what extent are assessment strategies encouraging collaborative problem-solving and team-building skills? To what extent are our assessment strategies facilitating meaningful, worthwhile learning outcomes from both the learner and the faculty perspectives?

Provide an Integrated System of Support

Granger and Benke remind us that a successful system to support learners begins with the prospective learner's first awareness and contact with our program to request information and it extends through graduation. Further, this learner support system should work in an integrated fashion to foster the learner's engagement and progress in his or her studies. One can't separate the process of registration, application for financial aid, acquisition of library resources, tutoring assistance, or counseling services from the design, delivery, and evaluation of teaching and learning, including faculty development and instructional technology support. Integration is key and we should strive to make it seamless. If you take the Granger-Benke challenge and walk through your system as a learner, how integrated is the support? Is it simple, efficient, and convenient? Where has the system of support failed to enable you to make progress toward your learning goals? Perhaps asking a few of your learners is another way to answer the same questions.

In the end, it seems appropriate to return to the Brown and Duguid (1996, p. 19) quote shared earlier that simply states: "Without more thought to learners and their practical needs, we fear that not only will [communications] technologies be underexploited, but they may well reinforce the current limitations of our higher education system." The challenge is clear. Are we equal to the task?

So, when it's all said and done, what does all this mean to those of us who'll enter the distance education classroom tomorrow? To those who are about to teach at a distance next semester? To those who are still debating whether or not to jump into the fray? Does it mean we can no longer do business as usual? Maybe and maybe not.

The message that seems to be conveyed by the authors is that we, as distance educators, need to be learner-centered reflective practitioners.

References

American Council on Education. (1996). *Guiding principles for distance learning in a learning society.* Washington, DC: Author

Brown, J.S. & Duguid, P. (1996). Universities in the digital age. *Change,* July/August, 11-19.

Resources

I've included a list of some of my favorite readings on distance education and the distance learner for those readers who might want to "read more about it." The list is by no means exhaustive nor was it meant to be. In addition, I have listed a number of journals that focus specifically on distance education and often highlight research on the learner at a distance. Three of my most favorite Web sites are also noted.

Books

Duning, B., Van Kekeris, M., & Zaborowski, L. (1993). *Reaching learners through telecommunications*. San Francisco: Jossey-Bass.

Evans, T., & Nation, D. (Eds.). (1989). *Critical reflections on distance education*. New York: The Falmer Press.

Garrison, D.R. (1989). *Understanding distance education: A framework for the future*. Boston: Routledge and Kegan Paul.

Harry, K., John, M., & Keegan, D. (Eds.). (1993). *Distance education: New perspectives*. London: Routledge.

Hodgson, V.E. (1987). *Beyond distance teaching: Towards open learning* Milton Keynes, England: The Open University.

Keegan, D. (Ed.). (1993). *Theoretical principles of distance education* London: Routledge.

Lockwood, F. (Ed.). (1995). *Open and distance learning today*. London: Routledge.

Moore, M. (Ed.). (1990). *Contemporary issues in American distance edu cation*. New York: Pergamon Press.

Moore, M., & Kearsley, G. (1996). *Distance education: A systems view*. Belmont, CA: Wadsworth Publishing Co.

Watkins, B., & Wright, S. (Eds.). (1991). *The foundations of American distance education: A century of collegiate correspondence study*. Dubuque, IA: Kendall/Hunt Publishing Co.

Wedemeyer, C. (1981). *Learning at the backdoor: Reflections on non-tra ditional learning in the lifespan*. Madison, WI: University of Wisconsin Press.

Willis, B. (1993). *Distance education: A practical guide*. Englewood Cliffs, NJ: Educational Technology Publications.

Willis, B. (1994). *Distance education: Strategies and tools*. Englewood Cliffs, NJ: Educational Technology Publications.

Journals and Newsletters

There are a number of journals that focus on research in distance education as well as newsletters that highlight this dynamic field. Several of my favorites are listed below. For additional sources, you might want to check one or more of the Web sites listed in the following section.

American Journal of Distance Education
American Center for the Study of Distance Education
Pennsylvania State University
403 S. Allen St., Suite 206
University Park, PA 16801-5202

The Journal of Distance Education
CADE Secretariat
151 Slater Street
Ottawa, Ontario
Canada K1P 5N1

Distance Education
Distance Education Centre
University College of Southern Queensland
PO Darling Heights

Toowoomba, Queensland 4350
Australia

Distance Education Report
Magna Publications, Inc.
2718 Dryden Drive
Madison, WI 53704-3086

World Wide Web Sites

Web sites are notorious for disappearing or for becoming rapidly out of date. Those listed below are ones I feel comfortable recommending for a number of reasons. First and foremost, they are tied to institutions with a history of commitment to distance education. These sites are closely monitored and updated on a regular basis. They highlight a wealth of resources, including conferences and workshops, funding sources, trends, data, and current issues. In addition, they provide selective links to other distance education and training-related sites.

A*DEC
http://www.adec.edu

The Distance Education Clearinghouse
http://www.uwex.edu.disted.home.html

International Center for Distance Learning
http://www-icdl.open.ac.uk/

Index

About the authors

Dr. Chère Campbell Gibson is Chair of the Graduate Program of Continuing and Vocational Education at the University of Wisconsin — Madison. She teaches courses on the adult independent learner, instructional design for distance learning, and issues in distance education. Her research focuses on the learner at a distance, with a specific emphasis on persistence and on the types of support that facilitate learning and completion. In addition, she has designed several award winning instructional packages, is a past Director of the University of Wisconsin System Extended Degree Programs, past Chair of the Teaching at a Distance Conference offered annually by the University of Wisconsin — Madison, and the originator of UW-Madison's Certificate of Professional Development in Distance Education.

Dr. Michael Moore is Academic Director of the American Center for the Study of Distance Education (ACSDE) at The Pennsylvania State University. He is the founder and editor of *The American Journal of Distance Education*. Since his 1972 theory of distance education — generally regarded as the first attempt in English to conceptualize and define this field of practice — Michael has advocated and explained distance education in numerous publications, presentations, workshops, and seminars throughout the world. From 1996 thorough 1998 Michael has been a visiting scholar and consultant at the World Bank with assignments to South Africa, Russia, Brazil, and Egypt.

Dr. **Melody M. Thompson** holds both a master's and doctoral degree in Adult Education from The Pennsylvania State University. She was a writer and editor for the American Center for the Study of Distance Education and is currently Assistant Director of Operations and Evaluation at Penn State's World Campus and a faculty member teaching Adult Education in the College of Education. Melody's teaching, research, and writing focus on distance education, the history of adult education, and diversity in adult education. Her most recent publication (with Michael Moore) is the 1997 *Effects of Distance Learning* (revised edition).

Dr. **Elizabeth Burge** is a Professor of Adult Education at the University of New Brunswick in Atlantic Canada. She says she tries to walk the talk of constructionist and common sense approaches to teaching and learning in adult and distance mode programs and in her M.Ed. classes, her writing, research and workshop activity. Liz is the 1997/98 Past President of the Canadian Association for Distance Education/Association Canadienne de l'education à distance. She has worked in distance education since 1978, and she led the development of an international group of women distance educators (WIN).

Dr. **Irene M. Sanchez** is the Bureau Chief for the Child Care Services Bureau of the New Mexico Children, Youth, and Families Department. She oversees child care assistance and licensing programs for the State and is responsible for overseeing a statewide program for the training of child care providers. She has an earned doctorate degree in Training and Learning Technologies from the University of New Mexico and has worked in public service agencies where she has extensive experience in program administration, staff development and training of professionals and para-professionals, specializing in multicultural education of adult learners.

Dr. **Charlotte N. (Lani) Gunawardena** is Associate Professor of Distance Education and Instructional Technology in the Organizational Learning and Instructional Technology Program at the University of New Mexico. She developed the graduate emphasis area in distance education at the University of New Mexico and has been active for the past decade in conducting research on distance education. Her current research interests center around design and evaluation of constuctivist learning environments facilitated by computer conferencing, social presence theory, and implications for interaction and communication, and the evaluation of distance education.

Dr. **Christine Olgren** is Distance Education Program Manager, Continuing and Vocational Education, University of Wisconsin-Madison. She is responsible for directing the Distance Education Certificate Program, the Annual Conference on Distance Teaching and Learning, and other professional development services. An author of over thirty books, articles and research reports in the field, Chris has worked in the field of distance education since 1977. Her experience includes program management, program development, instructional design, marketing, technology assessment, student advising, and instruction via audio, video, and the Internet.

Dr. **Terry Anderson** is currently the Director of Academic Technologies for Learning (ATL) at the University of Alberta (htp://www.atl.ualberta.ca) and is also an Associate Professor in the Faculty of Extension. His research interests relate to development and evaluation of WWW support for distance and classroom delivery and in the use of electronic communication tools to support "virtual" professional development activities. Terry was the Director of Contact North, a distance education delivery network in Northern Ontario and he coordinated what was probably the first "virtual conference" on the Internet, the Bangkok Project, of the International Council on Distance Education in 1992.

Currently, Dr. **Randy Garrison** holds the position of Dean, in the Faculty of Extension, at the University of Alberta. He previously held the position of Associate Dean (Research and Development) in the Faculty of Continuing Education and Director of Distance Education at the University of Calgary. There he developed a very successful Master's degree specializing in workplace learning that was accessible to working professionals globally. His areas of research are related to the teaching and learning transaction in the context of adult, distance, and higher education. He has published extensively in these areas.

Dr. **Daniel Granger** is currently the Director of Distributed Learning and Extended Education at California State University, Monterey Bay. He has been in distance education for twenty years, previously serving as the Director of Distance Education at the University of Minnesota and as Director of the Center for Distance Learning at SUNY Empire State College. He has written and spoken extensively on distance education from the learner perspective, and he currently serves on the editorial boards of *Open Learning* and the *Distance Education Report* He edited the special issue on "Distance Education in North America" of *Open Praxis* (Vol. 1, 1997), the journal of the International Council on Distance Education.

Dr. **Meg Benke** has been with Empire State College since 1990 and connected with distance education since 1983. Her work in education has focused on the connections between work, employers, and education. In addition to teaching in the graduate and undergraduate programs, in the areas of adult educational policy, leadership, human resource development, and training and learning organizations, Meg also studies outcomes for students in distance learning and the assessments of prior learning. Since coming to Empire State College, Meg has written and presented primarily in the areas of learner supports for distance learners and employer sponsored distance learning.